Extraordinary Leadership

Other Books by Roberta M. Gilbert, M.D.

*Extraordinary Relationships: A New Way of Thinking
About Human Interactions*

*Connecting With Our Children: Guiding Principles for
Parents in a Troubled World*

*The Eight Concepts of Bowen Theory: A New Way of
Thinking About The Individual and The Group*

EXTRAORDINARY LEADERSHIP

*Thinking Systems,
Making a Difference*

by

Roberta M. Gilbert M.D.

Leading Systems Press
Falls Church & Basye, Virginia

2nd Printing 2009

For additional copies of this book
and to inquire about quantity discounts,
contact:

Business Manager
Leading Systems Press
Center for the Study of Human Systems
313 Park Avenue, Suite 308
Falls Church VA 22046
or call 703 532-3823

See also www.hsystems.org

Table of Contents

This book is dedicated to clergy people who have learned and taught in the seminars about the usefulness of systems thinking in the congregational setting.

FOREWORD

How I got into the ministry

When asked, several years ago, by a leader in a major denomination to design a program for the clergy, I wondered what I had to offer. I was not a clergy person, but a psychiatrist. Though ministers made up a preponderance of my practice, I felt ill-equipped to meet their needs in a formal program. I could only guess at all the sticky issues they might bring in. Further, I didn't understand their organizations' structures very well. They were all a bit different—how could I learn them all? Still, I had consulted to enough clergy people to know that I was able to be a useful resource for most of the questions they brought to me. And anyway, their dilemmas did not revolve around the structures of their organizations.

I wrestled with these issues for a long time and, at last, realized that I did have something to offer, and it was very important. I could teach them to *"think systems."*

My experience with clergy and other leaders had shown that systems thinking was exactly what they desperately needed. *I decided that I would try to devise a way for them to obtain the purest and most accessible form of family systems theory that I could.* I need not know the exact size and shape of their problems—they would teach me that.[1]

With this decided, I became motivated and energized. The elements of the program fell quickly into place. "Extraordinary Leadership Seminar" would be a three year curriculum—it takes time to work on self and change old ways of interacting. Not everyone would be able to stay for three years, but that would be

---

[1] An idea presented by Dr. Dan Papero at the Bowen Center for the Study of the Family in his work with business leadership several years ago.

an ideal beginning for those serious about learning to think systems. The program would make use of the rich reservoir of experienced, brilliant teachers in the Washington D.C. area. Each year would repeat the basics, but each year would be different. Several other guiding principles, adopted at the beginning, have served extremely well.

Over time, the seminar grew to three separate sections, all in Virginia. Two of the sections meet one day a month, nine times during the academic year. One section meets three times a year, three days each time, so that people can travel to it from a distance. They all utilize illustrated lectures, discussion, videotapes, DVD's and both group and individual coaching.

It has been more than gratifying to see how the pastors of several denominations and faiths (and a number of non-clergy professionals) have made use of the systems thinking they have been able to absorb in these sessions. The overwhelmingly positive evaluations at the end of each year and rapid progress in people's life functioning greatly exceeded expectations for one so new to the field of leadership training.

Or, was I new to the field? With further thought, I could see that I was not at all. I had been coaching parents, *the leaders of the nuclear family*, for many years. I had seen the same positive feedback and exciting results there, too—just not as fast. The theory guiding my efforts, Bowen family systems theory, is the same for parents as for other leaders. And so parents become an important paradigm for leadership.

Most leaders and their coaches have few if any guiding principles to help with the intricacies and emotional intensities that are characteristic of organizations today. But, when I had seen families pull up in their functioning, losing symptoms and doing better than they ever had, it was with the guidance of Bowen theory. The same held true of my own family experience. I don't delude myself that I have mastered all that Bowen theory contains about relationships—family or otherwise. I will be working on that the rest of my life. I do believe, however, that I have learned something about what is needed to get to better relationships. And the guidelines for becoming a better functioning parent are, to my way of thinking, identical with those that leaders need in order to think through the most knotty problem confronting them—the emotional side of the organization.[2] Moreover, the ideas point the way toward becoming the best kind of leader possible in any system; what I term "high level," or Extraordinary Leaders.

A new way of thinking

When one organization circulated and read *Extraordinary Relationships*,[3] one of its members told the author that people in it were saying, "This is going to change the way we do everything!" Though this realization can be intimidating to some, the comment showed they were getting the message of the book. Change is one of the consequences of thinking systems. Indeed, there are profound consequences in adopting "a new way of thinking."

What is all the excitement about? It can be attributed to the impact of the life and work of Dr. Murray Bowen, a psychiatrist who lived between 1913 and 1990. He developed the useful and paradigm-shattering ideas of "Bowen family systems theory" during his early professional years at the famous Menninger Clinic, then in Topeka, Kansas. He saw that the existing study of the human, which then was based on what people thought and subjective interpretations of what clients said on the couch, was neither objective nor subject to replication. This approach, he thought, was unlikely to bring psychiatry into the realm of science. Thus, he decided to break away from the traditional theory and *to devise a new theory, based on observations that could, in time, enable the study of the human to become a science.* Once he could see that the family and not the individual, was the proper unit of study, as well as several corollaries

---

[2] See volume of the same name, published by the Bowen Center for the Study of the Family.

[3] Roberta M. Gilbert, *Extraordinary Relationships,* John Wiley and Sons, New York, 1992.

derived from that premise, he had a theory. And it was one that he thought could some day become documented as fact, corroborated by scientific study. He devoted the rest of his life to developing and expanding the theoretical ideas. During his research years at the National Institutes of Health and teaching, practicing and writing at Georgetown University School of Medicine and the Georgetown Family Center (now the Bowen Center for the Study of the Family) he became, over time, only more convinced of the veracity of what he had discovered in those early years at Menninger.

From the beginning, Dr. Bowen was a "consummate teacher." He always had a group of learners gathered around or following him around.[4] That pattern was to continue throughout his life. I was one of the lucky ones who gathered around, beginning in 1981, absorbing all I could from him and his faculty at "Georgetown," as the center is known in shorthand. In time, I was privileged to become a member of that faculty, an honor I count higher than most others.

Bowen described a continual effort of working on himself to be a better leader in all his groups, whether family or work.[5, 6] His efforts on his own functioning positively affected the organizations he led. In this way he learned that the ideas, so helpful to families, were actually useful to all groups (systems) of humans.

A theory about leadership

Bowen family systems theory is, among many other things, about leadership. Those who have taken on its challenges, working with its principles over years of time, have found that it

---

[4] Personal communication from a psychiatrist whose mentor was Dr. Bowen when he himself was in training at Menninger.

[5] See the "Commemorative" tape of Bowen's life work created by Andrea Maloney Schara,, the Bowen Center for the Study of the Family.

[6] Bowen, M., *Family Therapy in Clinical Practice,* Aronson, New York, 1978, p.461 ff.

is a demanding taskmaster. It takes us to lonely, frustrating, tense and even *counterintuitive* places. Yet we find ourselves becoming more solid, principled, useful, interesting, creative, and productive over the long term. We see the groups of which we are a part, beginning with our own families, functioning better. We would not go back to the old ways of thinking for anything.

It is, as Bowen noted, an attractive place. People gather around us in a way they did not before. As we begin the work, first with our families of origin, proceeding to the families we have created and moving on to other important systems, we gradually discover that, increasingly, we get asked what we think, or to perform special tasks for groups that no one else can do as well. In short, *Bowen theory nudges people slowly but surely into positions of leadership.*

Thinking systems, people take the time and effort to find out what it is they believe about a given situation or predicament, based on well-studied and understood principles, and then let others know about it (define themselves) when that is appropriate. This effort to stand emotionally apart from the system *while remaining in good contact with it* is different. People take note. They may not agree with one at all times. They may even react, at times, as one changes. But they are intrigued. And if one stays on course, thoughtful and connected to important people in the system, one stands to see the whole system rise up to a higher level of functioning. That is leadership of the highest and best order.

In one's family, when relating as the best one can be with the generation before or with one's offspring, there is an expectation of self to know what one thinks and represent that, when it becomes important. *Being the best one can be in one's relationship systems is extraordinary leadership.* And that family paradigm, representing one's best thinking, guided by systems thinking, whether as a grownup offspring or as a parent in the family, is one that can be returned to again and again to try to understand what principled leadership looks like.

At a feeling level, most of us may be unsure that we know much about difficult family relationships. By any standard, they are complex. We have all botched them often. At any given time, they may not feel completely satisfying. Yet, it is in those family relationships that all the principles, and much of the learning, for extraordinary leadership reside. So if one can begin to understand the family, one can understand any human system. That complex organism, the organization, can begin to make sense and one can find a way to conduct oneself according to observed and tested principles *that work toward better functioning of both the self and the organization.*

Clergy as key leaders

Why single out the clergy among leaders of organizations? For two reasons. First, this is where my experience working with non-family leaders was acquired.

Second, along with Dr. Karl Menninger, one of America's most important psychiatrists, I believe the clergy could be key to leading Western society out of the quagmire it now finds itself in. He believed so strongly that recognizing our part in the world transgression was the only remaining hope that he wrote a book about this.[7] He thought that all the rest of us should support and assist the clergy in this most important responsibility of helping us to help ourselves.

It is apparent to me that our society is in trouble. It is, as authors Strauss and Howe of the *Fourth Turning,* put it, "unraveling."[8] Bowen saw it coming in the 1960's.[9]

Menninger also saw it. He thought that the major responsibility in lifting society to a better level was the clergy's. But he regretted that the clergy was minimizing its great

---

[7] Menninger, K, *Whatever Became of Sin?*, Hawthorn Books, New York, 1973, p. 220.
[8] Strauss, W and Howe, N, *The Fourth Turning,* Broadway, 1997, New York, p.1, 7, 21, 22.
[9] Stated in his lectures at Georgetown.

traditional and historical opportunity "to preach, to prophesy, to speak out."

If a critical mass of leaders ever grasps the ideas contained within family systems theory, takes them seriously and puts them into practice, I believe there will be a significant impact for the better on a society that is now deep into regression. I believe we might even find a way to pull ourselves up and out of the downward spiral, circumventing what some believe to be our impending species suicide.

As Bowen put it: ". . . *the biological-instinctive-feeling oriented part of man will not provide consistent help in finding solutions: and . . . constructive solutions . . . will depend on the highest functioning of intellectual man in directing total man toward solutions.*"[10]

Guidebooks for leadership

Now, after several years' experience with the Extraordinary Leadership Seminar, comes another principal text for the program. The text for the second year, *The Eight Concepts of Bowen Theory,* was written first because of its projected wider application. It has been received enthusiastically by many clergy people, therapists, professors, parents and others. Because the seminar was planned as a three year program, however, three texts are needed, one for each year. The present book is designed to accompany the first year of the seminar training. A text for the third year is planned to follow.

To avoid unnecessary repetition in the texts, the formal presentation of Bowen theory is contained as a unified whole in *The Eight Concepts of Bowen Theory.* The three books will be complementary, intended to be used together. Thus, in reading *Extraordinary Leadership,* the reader may, from time to time, find it useful to review various chapters in *The Eight Concepts* that provide amplification of the different concepts.

---

[10] Bowen, *Family Therapy,* op. cit., p. 447b.

Bowen family systems theory is a most useful set of ideas for those in a leadership position. *The theory gives us a view of something about which most of us learned nothing at all in our training—emotional systems and how they work.* Clergy people constantly reiterate that their education in no way addresses or prepares them for the intensity and turbulence of the emotional side of the congregations they serve. People in other professions say something similar. The ideas contained in the theory help us understand high and low level functioning in leadership and in life in general. Thus, they challenge us always to do better and then show us how. They help us understand our families and ourselves. The ideas make us more accepting of everyone. They show us how to conduct ourselves in relationships in ways that are useful rather than destructive to them. It is my hope that more and more people over time will find out about the ideas presented here and in other writings[11] and programs around the country[12] and begin to use them in their lives.

There are many books on leadership.[13] They are written from a variety of theoretical perspectives. This book is based on a "new way of thinking" that sees the group as the emotional unit. This new way of thinking sets the present text apart from other books on leadership. Most of them are quite complex, loaded with categories and categories within categories. They are full of advice. With the new way of thinking, or new lens through which we see the system, however, it becomes unnecessary to teach people how to lead, find out what kind of personality they have or to administer tests to "determine" the personalities in the group. It is only necessary to learn about the emotional functioning of groups, individuals, and self—family systems theory is really devoid of a lot of the usual categories. It

---

[11] See Appendix II for a basic bibliography in Bowen family systems theory.

[12] See Appendix III for a listing of some of the centers that offer various types of programs.

[13] See Romig, D., *Side By Side Leadership,* for a summary of the major contemporary work on the subject. Bard Press, Austin, Atlanta, 2001, pp. 37, 38.

is not terribly complex.[14] The theory itself points the way, so there is less analysis to perform and little "how to" involved.

Through that lens of Bowen theory, the individual is put into perspective. He or she is part of something much larger than self. This way of thinking does not assign blame, try to find "causes" or interpret "why" people do what they do. It accepts that people, under the influence of anxiety, can become quite— interesting! And then, it watches.

Because repetition is a proven teacher (and because not everyone can stay in the seminar for three years) there is built-in redundancy in the program. Because the books follow the plan of the seminar, there is some repetition of ideas in the texts, too.

Each idea presented in this book is presented first as it was discovered, in the human family and other natural systems.[15] After that, each is expanded upon to show how it works in larger organizations. It is much easier to start from the simpler and extrapolate to the more complex than to jump right into trying to comprehend the emotional side of organizations without a grounding in the smaller and easier-to-understand family system.

Because I believe the prototype of "parent" is so useful for leaders, it is a big part of this book. In fact, whenever I use the word "leaders" I am referring to parents and pastors as well as all leaders in whatever setting. Bowen theory is the same for all and equally useful for all. Most seminar participants to date have been ministers, but there have also been lay leaders in congregations, educators, counselors, business executives as well as the leaders of the family, parents. If leaders in settings other than congregations find the thinking useful, so much the better.

This book will consider leadership in three parts. Part 1 considers The System. Another word descriptive of emotional systems is "togetherness." It describes how anxiety affects

---

[14] For a brief explanation of the formal concepts of Bowen theory, see Gilbert, R., *The Eight Concepts of Bowen Theory,* Leading Systems Press, Falls Church, VA, 2004.

[15] For a fuller explanation of the ideas of the theory itself, see *The Eight Concepts of Bowen Theory, op. cit.*

groups and individuals and the relationship patterns we see when groups are emotionally stirred up. It also takes up congregations as emotional systems and guidelines for leaders within them. It then examines the biological and instinctual basis for hierarchy.

Part II looks at The Self, or "Individuality." Here, we start by thinking about the amazing degrees of variation that exist in humans. Next, it considers what high level relationship functioning is—"extraordinary relationships." We see how this spectrum of human functioning challenges us all to do better as individuals. We look at how the spectrum itself defines high and low level leadership and how parents become an analogy for leadership; specifically, clergy leadership. Then, since leaders have to be excellent public communicators, we consider speaking and writing, as viewed through the lens of Bowen family system theory.

Part III puts it all together in "The Self in the System." It looks at today's systems with their intense issues. It examines clergy as leaders in today's world, clergy as counselors, the very special functions of clergy and the unique place the clergy hold in society. It will conclude by demonstrating how theory has been confirmed over and over during the Extraordinary Leadership clergy seminars.

The epilogue brings together a variety of surprise lessons the author has learned over the course of many Extraordinary Leadership seminars.

In all the examples used in the text, identifying details have been altered.

I do not see this small volume as the last or best word on Bowen theory. It is merely my understanding of some of the basic, beginning ideas as they apply to leadership.

Come with me, then, on a journey of systems thinking about leadership. I offer the invitation with the hope that the ideas will be of as much continued use in this printed form as they seem to have been "live."

PART I

THE SYSTEM

—TOGETHERNESS

"In an anxiety field the group moves toward more togetherness to relieve the anxiety."

"The togetherness forces defined family members as being alike in terms of important beliefs, philosophies, life principles and feelings . . . The forces constantly emphasize the togetherness by using 'we' to define what 'we think or feel,' or . . . define the self of another."

". . . emotional forces overlap and bind together . . ."

Source for quotes on preceding page: Murray Bowen, *Family Therapy and Clinical Practice*, Aronson, 1978, pp. 277, 218, 294

|

Emotional Systems and How They Work

Leaders taken by surprise

Clergy people, for the most part, are wonderful people. They are intelligent, sensitive, and idealistic. When they graduate from seminary they approach their duties full of creativity and energy. Their hopes and dreams include devoting their lives to helping people in the service of God. They work incredible numbers of hours serving their congregations. But they have no idea what, sooner or later, awaits them. For most, there is a rude reality waiting in the shadows that is totally unexpected. It seems to come at them from out of the blue—and it is unpleasant.

What they find is that the emotional side of the congregation, that supportive, loving, and caring side, can also flip, becoming negative, perplexing, and difficult to manage. It can turn against the minister or rabbi, becoming critical or vindictive. It can spare the leader, but stir up the congregation to an extent that nothing useful can get accomplished. It can obstruct forward progress of any kind. Clergy people are usually completely blindsided by it.

The pastor may wonder "What course in seminary ever prepared me for this?" or think, "I never dreamed it would be this way," or simply leave the ministry in terror or other unmanageable emotional reactions, never to return. Some statistics estimate that 40% of clergy leave the field in the first five years after the completion of their seminary training. While not all of these leave for emotional reasons, it is a safe bet that a large number do. Clergy, as well as most professionals, are given no way of thinking about the emotional side of organizations. Thus, when it shows up, intense and negative, they are unable to deal with it.

Good news for leaders

The emotional side of the congregation, and how clergy people deal with it, is precisely what the author has been observing in the past few years. Though there is still much to learn, much has been learned. And it turns out that the effective tools found in family systems theory that have been so useful for many years to so many families are incredibly useful for leaders of congregations and other organizations as well.

The tools are not particularly intuitive. *They run counter to much that has already been taught and learned.* Therefore, they take time to acquire. The good news is that they can be. And over time, one gets better and better at using them. They amount to "a new way of thinking" about the human. In time, one gains a lens that affords a bigger and better picture of human events. A more accurate view makes it possible to respond to the emotional side of organizations in a way that is useful to it and also to the leader. In time, people working at "seeing through the new lens" actually experience less wear and tear as a result of their efforts, gaining renewed energy and confidence.

Within this simple (in some ways) yet complex (in others) way of seeing are derived guidelines for relationships; managing self within emotional fields—by far the most important keys to leadership success. As people gain that knowledge, they automatically learn their own strengths and weaknesses. Theory itself shows what they are, and then, by their own efforts, with coaching, over time, they step up in their leadership ability. They step up because by far most of the difficulty leaders experience is in relationships. With a new way of seeing—Bowen family systems theory—they understand more clearly how relationships work well and how they get off track. They see what their part in a stuck relationship is. If they learn to "think systems," leaders don't need typical classes or books on how to be a good leader. Family systems theory points the way, and if they take it seriously, applying it in their lives, they automatically become better and better leaders, on a continuing basis, the rest of their lives.

This is not to say that applying the ideas is easy. The human changes only slowly and with much kicking and screaming. That is why it takes time, effort, teaching, reading and coaching. The "new way of thinking" is *new*, to most of us[1], and it takes time to learn it, drop other opposing, ingrained teachings (traditional theory about the human) and grow the countless numbers of new neural connections involved in such an effort. But in a relatively short period of time, people begin to see the changes in themselves that they are looking for. Others see them, too. And, it is not a matter of giving or taking advice, except for the adage: *"Learn theory, learn theory, learn theory—if you learn theory you can use it. If you don't you can't."* The systems theory itself gives the advice and shows the way.

Now let's start by taking a look at what emotional systems are, how they work and how an understanding of them changes the way we think about almost everything.

Family, the model for understanding

Since the family is the model for the organization, parents become an important homologue for leadership. The ideas were first discovered in the family. But more important, if we understand how a family functions as an "emotional unit," then we can expand to the greater complexities of the organization. If we know how high functioning parents operate, we'll know more about high functioning leadership.

---

[1] Some probably have more, and others, less, ability to think systems.

In addition, much of the behavior people exhibit in organizations is patterned in that original group, one's own family, so there is no way we can understand group behavior without understanding the family first. Further, much of the most important work of the best functioning leaders is done on themselves in their families—the ones they grew up in as well as the one they helped create. As they work to change their patterned functioning, their responses and behavior become less automatic and more the result of choice.

So, for all these reasons, as complete an understanding of the human family as possible is essential. In describing and heading towards better functioning as leaders in organizations we always begin with how the ideas play out in the family.

Emotional systems—"togetherness"

The most important fact about families is that they constitute an emotional unit. Though most of us think of the individual as the unit, it is, rather, the nuclear family as a group that, for systems thinkers, constitutes the emotional whole. *What affects one affects all in that unit.* The family is bound by an emotional "togetherness" that is like glue. If one person in a family is upset, the entire unit is upset to some degree. Thus, *anxiety originating in one circulates throughout the family unit.*[2]

In a herd of cattle, for instance, such as the ones my grandfathers kept, if one of the cows became upset for some reason, such as receiving a shock from the electric fence, or seeing a snake, they would all become upset and move closer together. The upset (anxiety) travels, almost instantaneously, through the entire herd. We call it the "herding" reaction. They are an emotional unit.

In the family, togetherness begins at or before birth. A baby, born into a human family, is totally dependent on its family for nurturance and interaction. It can do very little to

---

[2] It is a convention in family systems theory to refer to intense emotion of whatever type, as anxiety. It is not necessary, for the purpose of thinking systems, to describe its shading (depression, elation, etc.).

support its life other than to call for attention through crying. Almost all its needs must be provided. If danger threatens or seems to, the anxious baby may cry more or the parents might "hover" more. In the best functioning families, its parents are attentive and responsive, but not overly so. Some mother-father-child units, however, become stuck at an inappropriate level of dependency (or reaction to it).

Fusions

At its best, the herding (togetherness) reaction in the human family is necessary and it is also useful. The interdependency and reactivity of one to another indicate a degree of togetherness called *"fusion." As we grow and develop, there is less and less togetherness. But, there is, in all of us, some of this togetherness—fusion—that does not get resolved by adulthood.*

This herding tendency, togetherness or fusion, is an early, elemental part of higher mammals, including humans, and happens not only at infancy, between mother and baby. It is also present in adults, to the degree that it is unresolved. So it becomes more apparent whenever danger threatens, or seems to. Because of the fusions, as anxiety rises, it circulates around the system, from one to another. In that way each self, to a degree, participates in each other self. We say that *self is actually traded*, passing back and forth between the members of a family. Self is not traded in less important relationships. And, just as anxiety can pass between the cells of our bodies, it also passes from individual to individual in a group. In that manner, where anxiety goes defines the emotional unit.

Fusions are more apparent when anxiety rises. *Anxiety also is a product of fusions.* So, while they are evidently meant to be protective mechanisms against anxious situations, *fusions, unresolved in adulthood, mean that relationships can create anxiety of their own.*

When anxiety rises, several protective physiological mechanisms click into place. When danger threatens, anxiety heightens and the reactions are predictable. There are the classic "fight or flight" reactions. In addition, some species "freeze" in the face of danger or anxiety. Others start to caretake (or become sexual, which may be a variant of the latter).

These reactions are seen in the human as well. In an emotional unit of the family, when the anxiety elevates, humans will tend to **fight:**

- Start an argument
- Criticize or
- Compete.

They may **flee:**

- Leave, emotionally or actually
- Change the subject, or
- Stop talking.

Or they may **freeze:**

- A part of the body stops working
- The brain stops working, or
- The individual becomes helpless or paralyzed.

Or, **caretake:**

- Have all the answers
- Dominate, or
- Do all the talking
- Worry about a third person.

These *postures* of emotional reactivity, when seen in the human emotional relationship system, the family, are called:

- **Conflict**
- **Distance** and its extreme,
- **Cutoff**

- **Overfunctioning/Underfunctioning Reciprocity** and
- **Triangling.**

These postures are meant to deal with the anxiety and, used short term, can reduce the amount of it. It is when they solidify into patterns—used long term—that they contribute more anxiety to the system. When that happens, they *add to the problem.*

These patterns, roughly equivalent to those seen in other species, are automatic when anxiety rises in groups. So, when we see them, we can take them as evidence that anxiety—and fusions—are present. Many people find that they have a favorite or usual way of reacting when the tension mounts. They may say;

- "You are the problem. If only you would change the way you. . ." (becoming *conflictual*), or

- "I'm outta here!" (*distancing* into the next room, actually cut off from the congregation, change professions or emigrate), or

- "Let me tell you what to do. . ." (*overfunctioning* into a superior, know-it-all, dominant stance) or

- "Help, I'm lost, tell me what to do." (*underfunctioning* by refusing to think or be a self in the situation) or

- "Say, what do you think?" *triangling* in a third person unnecessarily—when the first two have barely begun to work on the issue. Or, "Let me help the two of you out," triangling again, instead of showing confidence in them to work it out. Or, "Do you know what I heard about *her?*"

Many people (perhaps most) alternate among the postures—using different postures at different times.

Leaders can and regularly do find themselves in one or more of these situations. Consider, for example, the following:

Conflict

In the conflict pattern, no one takes responsibility for self. This is a reciprocal blaming, accusing posture in which each sees the other as the problem. It rarely leads to resolution of anything, since no one stops to think or is willing to look at self and work on his or her contribution—the only way a change can come about.[3]

Pastor A had a hot temper. Further, whenever someone disagreed with him, he took it as a personal insult. Many conversations that he saw as disagreements were simply people trying to say what they thought. By his automatic combative, competitive posture, however, he often unnecessarily escalated the emotional climate into conflict. He was not well-liked. Nothing got done in his congregation. He moved from one position to another frequently and people saw him as "the problem." The way he saw it, the others were always the instigators, malcontents or trouble-makers.

He did not realize how his posture of conflict was contributing to his problems.

When he began to work on becoming less reactive—a thinking presence in escalating or tense situations—they did not go on to conflict. People were able to continue to problem-solve and think their way to solutions and take appropriate action. Instead of avoiding him, people asked what he thought about issues.

One of the most interesting observations is the manner in which people beginning to think systems are able to see their

---

[3] In traditional theory, the focus is on blame or cause and effect. In family systems theory the focus is on what is happening and how one can, by changing self, make it different and better. The only person one can change is self. Because we are always dealing with an emotional unit, and each of us is only a part of it, *no one* is to blame. We all contribute to whatever is going on and by altering the role of self, change will likely follow. The focus, thus, becomes what is happening, what role one is playing and how to modify that role so as to bring about a better relationship.

own postures, as well as their consequences. The theory holds up a mirror to them in which they can see themselves in action.

Distance

Tiring of conflict, relationships can withdraw into distance, for relief. Distance may be a reaction to a family pattern of conflict. Or, circumstances may seem to force a distancing posture, as with Pastor B.

Rev. B had, in one year, three funerals and a wedding in her family. One of the funerals was for her mother and the wedding, her son's. All of this called her out of the congregation a lot. When she was there, sometimes she was not really "there." Her mind was preoccupied with the major family events she was experiencing.

During this time, her congregation became embroiled in conflict over trivial issues. She was afraid and felt hopeless, not knowing what to do. Eventually the intensity of the group focused on her and she was seen as the problem. Indeed, unaware, she did contribute to it. They wanted her to leave so they could call someone else.

With coaching, she became calmer and more thoughtful. She began to meet regularly with the most intense members of the congregation, listening and *making calm contact*. They calmed down. Shortly after this, the whole congregation did also. They began to think constructively.

Later, she was able to lead them to solve a financial problem that had plagued the congregation for years. They paid their debts and found ways to live within their budget, having a grand time doing it. They begged her not to leave, though the time eventually came when she needed to. Pastor B eventually became known in her wider network as someone who could work wonders with difficult congregations.

When one can take responsibility for one's own part in emotional intensities, doing his or her own part differently, they gradually subside.

Cutoff

Those who react against intense situations by leaving the ministry entirely, are often people who have a pattern of cutting off from important relationships. Cutoff is the extreme form of the distance pattern and one does not have to look long or far to find it in church and synagogue today.

Rev, H, who had left a marriage that was distant by cutting off into divorce, had no idea how to handle criticism or complaints. When he encountered either he withdrew into depression, which led to inefficiency at his work. In several positions, when anything he perceived to be an "attack" was mounted, he had no idea how to address the problem. He would leave the position rather than talk things over with those who had concerns.

With coaching he learned a different way of responding to critical people. He would evaluate whether people's anxiety was triggered by his own anxious posture or behavior. If there were valid concerns about him, he could learn something and work on change. If they were unfounded—that is, they were more about the complainer than himself—he could realize that, connect with those involved, not react, and go on. He learned he didn't have to be decimated by criticism or other intensities, retreating into yet another cutoff. He could be present with it and work toward resolution of the anxiety.

Cutoff is so much a part of the world we live in that it can be hard to recognize. It feels wonderful in the beginning. One is rid of the problem. But cutoff does not solve anything. Only later do anxiety and often, symptoms, set in as emotional reactivity increases. *Because the negative symptoms of cutoff appear so long after the initial cutoff, they don't get identified with it.* For many of us, it is a part of our generations. But when we see it for what it is, we can begin to work on our cutoff tendencies. The rewards for this kind of effort are great.

Overfunctioning/underfunctioning reciprocity

In over- and underfunctioning reciprocal relationships, the overfunctioner, or dominant partner feels good and does well. The other one takes on anxiety as a result of this arrangement and, eventually, develops symptoms. *The dominant one gains self from the other, who loses it.*[4]

Rev. C, a brilliant mind, who truly did know many of the answers, had a congregation that said it wanted to grow—it was in a growing community. But it never did. It actually did nothing. The more Rev. C came up with ideas, answers and plans, the less the rest of the group did. He ran the church.

He, an only child, had never learned how to interact with others toward a common goal. His overfunctioning pattern meant that his wife was an underfunctioner. Because of his being so over-adequate and all-knowing, there was no room in the relationship for her to be a self. She was either sick or depressed most of the time.

When he saw how reciprocities in relationships work, and began to work on his part of them, things changed. He worked on seeing himself as, and being, more of an equal in his family relationships as well as his professional ones—giving others more room to be important, have ideas and actually interact as equals with him. They began to take on some of the responsibility for where things were going—it was an actual relief to him not to have to do everything. The congregation exhibited new energy for ideas and action. The underfunctioners in all his systems did better and the congregation started to grow.

When the overfunctioner gains more basic self,[5] it is not necessary to grab self from others. The leader does well, and the others do too.

---

[4] The concept of basic self is explained more fully in Part II.
[5] More about basic self and pseudoself in Part II.

Triangling

The ever-present tendency, in relationships, to bring in a third, or for one to try for more closeness when on the "outside" of two important others, in relationships, means that the original two end up not being direct with each other. They are absorbed with the third. Anxiety circulates around the triangle. It never calms down.

Triangles are not good or bad. They are simply a fact of life in all human systems. Triangles are a more stable way of managing anxiety than two-person relationships, because the anxiety between two in the triangle can always flow to the third, relieving the pressure. They are ubiquitous. It is not really a matter of getting out of them; rather, we need to learn to navigate within them. *They are so much a fact of life that all of human society is built on triangles.*

Rabbi D found that there always seemed to be rumors circulating in her congregation. Her friends would come and tell her what was being said, however, so she was not completely out of the loop. Often she found that a simple conversation with the most anxious, the instigators of the rumors, was enough to bring it to an end. (The conversation rarely was about the "issue." It was simply a way of making contact.) Sometimes she found a humorous way to address "the rumor of the week" from the pulpit. A good laugh was had by all—dissipating the anxiety—and the rumor was over.

In a group where anxiety continually circulates around the triangles, as it does in all but the highest level groups, people talk *about* each other rather than *to* each other, directly resolving their anxieties. Since anxiety that circulates usually escalates, the organization lives in varying degrees of intensity. *When people become more responsible for their feeling states, dealing directly with each other from a calmer, more thoughtful posture, this can change.* The leader can set the pace for that.

Making contact

Common to resolution of all these situations is the importance of the leader's learning to make calm contact with anxiety in the group. The emotional state of the leader has a tremendous effect upon any group. So when the leader can make contact with the more anxious ones, bringing his or her best thinking to bear, after the concerns have been heard, usually the anxiety will dissipate. Making calm contact has the effect of:

- Helping the leader to define self according to principle

- Letting the group bring out its best thinking

- Finding resolution for dilemmas

- Energizing individuals in the group and, eventually,

- A more energized group going toward action plans and follow through.

What it takes to change a pattern

It only takes one to change a relationship pattern. One person, seeing the emotional process and thinking systems, beginning to focus on the contribution of self to the pattern and changing that, can dissolve the whole pattern. Because both people in the relationship contribute to the pattern and because they are part of an emotional system, if one changes, the pattern will change. But, if anxiety is not resolved, the change can sometimes include simply changing from one pattern to another, as when people in conflict become tired of the conflict, retreating into distance. *Replacing a pattern with another pattern will provide no resolution of the anxiety.*

A leader, understanding relationship patterns and identifying them, can then address the anxiety behind them in the way he or she manages self. By refusing the relationship postures of the group, the leader can show a different way of relating that can be a step toward resolving the intense, reactive circulation of anxiety in the group.

Changing the way we think about everything

Once we see how we are all a part of a larger unit—the family—and that the patterns or postures are not good or bad, but rather simply a part of the human phenomenon, we can begin to observe more calmly, letting go of blame, censure, and hostility. We stop making diagnoses and trying to figure out who is at fault. Observation is key to understanding what is happening in the system and managing oneself well in it. The observing thinking leader becomes curious, engaged, and open to new learning. Energy previously tied up in negative feeling states is freed. Once this happens, many positive effects take place in body, mind—and in leadership!

Further, family systems theory informs us as to what next steps would be to get to better functioning for the self and for the group. It tells the high level leader how to proceed up and out of the stucknesses that so often confound groups of people important to each other.

Thinking It Over

The emotional system, formed by the "togetherness force" in all emotional systems and, in each of us, means that we are a part of something much larger than any individual—our systems, our emotional units. We are stuck together in fusions. What affects one person in the emotional unit, affects all. This idea changes the way we approach all human relationships.

Real Life Research

1. What are the relationship patterns that characterize an emotional system?

2. What relationship patterns were common in the family you grew up in?

3. Can you remember specific stories to illustrate them?

4. Are they still being replayed in your family?

5. Do you tend to fall back on one of the relationship patterns more of the time when anxiety goes up?

6. What is fusion?

7. Can you see your family emotional system experience playing out in your professional life?

8. How could you address your patterns in some of your important relationships in your original family? In your nuclear family?

9. Why are triangles important?

10. Why doesn't it work to replace one pattern with another?

11. What does it take to change a pattern?

2

Congregations as Emotional Systems

Congregations are like families

Congregations are not families and should not be referred to as such. In writing about organizations, Bowen thought that using the word "family" for organizations or encouraging a "happy family" attitude in them only encouraged those who are trying to get emotional needs met there inappropriately. *"There are those who refer to the work relationship system as a 'family.' My thesis is that it might be similar to a family, but it is* not *a family."*[1]

But families and non-family groups are like each other in some ways. How are organizations similar to a family? *Congregations or any other organizations show many of the same characteristics of emotional systems as do families.* Given enough anxiety, they all exhibit conflict, distance, cutoff, overfunctioning/underfunctioning reciprocity and triangling. That is because, like a family, at least to some extent, they are emotional systems.

---

[1] Bowen, M., *Family Therapy in Clinical Practice*, Jason Aronson, 1985, p. 462.

What does it take to form an emotional system? It takes simply *spending time together*. If the people in any group rub up against each other enough, we begin to see conflict—attempts to relieve the conflict by distancing—as well as all the other emotionally-based patterns humans show in important relationships. So, though not families, organizations do form emotional systems.

Further, we can see hierarchy develop in groups that spend time together. There will be leaders and there will be followers. This is not good or bad, it is simply a fact of life. When humans are in a group, it does not take long to see who emerges as leaders. It is obvious who is going along with them, more as followers. When we see that, or other relationship postures, we can assume that an emotional unit has been, or is being formed. The people are becoming important to each other by virtue of spending time together. Hierarchy is a special form of the overfunctioning/underfunctioning pattern that runs throughout a group, along with the other postures, especially when anxiety runs higher.[2]

When anxiety increases, for whatever reason, the relationship postures are more in evidence. They are, after all, attempts to resolve anxiety. Triangles, for example, during times of more stress, will be inevitable—rumors and gossip will abound. If the tension is high enough, anxiety will spill outside the original triangles and start forming new ones. These will build on each other and interlock. If an issue gets attached to them, they can polarize, with different factions taking sides. Such a phenomenon can fracture a group.

So, though they are similar in many ways to families, organizations are not families. One way they differ is that they are more complex. For one thing, they are usually larger than nuclear families. For another, they—especially congregations—contain many different families within them. So congregations, once the members have spent enough time together to become

---

[2] More about hierarchy in Chapter 4.

important to each other, have *emotional units within emotional units.*

Not only that, in small or large congregations there are still other smaller emotional units. These are the committees, boards, staff or the choir—any small group that meets together regularly. So they become smaller emotional units within the larger group. They might be called "virtual families." They become emotionally important to each other simply by spending more time together than does the rest of the group.

Leaders need time together

Just as parents set the emotional tone for the emotional unit of the family, leaders set it for the organization. If parents do not make enough time for each other, or have a relationship that doesn't work in other ways, there will be unresolved anxiety in their relationship that can affect everyone in their family. In the same way, if leaders neglect taking time to resolve issues, to plan, to understand each other's thinking, or get themselves into anxious patterns, their relationships will generate unresolved anxiety that cannot help but spread throughout the congregation.

Leaders in their own families

In addition, because the emotional tone of the leader is influential, if the family relationships of the pastor are disturbed or distant, he or she will carry around a load of anxiety that will automatically permeate the entire organization. But, early on, Bowen discovered that those who took their patterns into their original families, working on them there, showed positive changes in their functioning. They got a superior result to anything seen before, even with years of therapy.

In their family work, leaders need to head toward the difficult relationships. We all have people in our families we would rather not relate to. But theory directs us toward them, to actually get a one-to-one relationship with them as much as to the "easier" ones. They are the ones, after all, that teach us more about managing ourselves in relationships than any others. The

21

easy, supportive relationships are useful too, and we all benefit from them. But the best leaders try to get a one-on-one relationship with as many people in their extended family system as possible. Most of our families exhibit a wide spectrum of functioning. Thus all these relationships give a broad view and experience of what family emotional process is.

Sometimes leaders don't recognize the family anxiety they habitually carry, until after working with it awhile. Over time, when their family relationships have improved considerably, they can look back and see and feel the difference. The best functioning leaders are always working on improving their relating ability in their original and nuclear families, trying to connect in a more meaningful way, staying out of the relationship patterns, making a point to be present and accounted for at important times and events in the life of the family. As they do this they find themselves enjoying life more.

Ten guidelines for high level leaders

The best leaders find, in Bowen family systems theory, *guidelines* that make a huge difference. Following are some that have emerged as particularly useful:

1. Keep in touch with all the families.

It is extremely important for anyone in a leadership role to be in regular contact with the different emotional systems of the group—the families and the "virtual" families. In a small congregation, this is not as difficult as in a large one, where it can seem impossible. In that case, making regular contact with the leadership of the various groups in the congregation, keeps the minister in contact with the whole emotional unit—as well as the units contained within it. Leaders who ignore this need for all parts of the organization to be in touch with him or her pay a price.

2. Bowen theory describes "ideal relationships."

They are **separate, equal, and open.**[3] The leader keeps **separate boundaries,** knowing what he or she can and cannot do, refusing off-loads of anxiety from others, not broadcasting anxiety to the group and not taking part in group emotional process. He or she takes responsibility for defining thinking when appropriate. The leader **communicates openly**—one aspect of integrity—out of his or her own thinking. This person is sought out, for conversation, guidance and counseling. He or she relates as an **equal** to others. Unlike the parent of a small child, (the parent analogy has its limits) he or she relates to everyone as a peer. There is no authoritarian domination here (a high functioning parent doesn't do that anyway), but when immaturity in the group threatens the group's functioning or disrespects it, this leader can say, "No."

3. See the triangles and address them.

Thinking theory, the best leaders can see triangles and addresses those participating in them rather than shying away from them in fear. Sometimes the angles need to be put together; "You two can work it out." Sometimes the central triangle-generating person or persons need to be addressed. It seems that one of the most efficient and frequent ways to generate interlocking triangles these days is by e-mail.

When Pastor E found that the whole congregation had been e-mailed a document about the church finances that was erroneous and fallacious, as evidence that the pastor should be fired, a friend informed him about what was going on. The pastor went to the document's author, the church treasurer, and said, "There will be an independent audit of the church's financial status next week. If this document is found to be in error, you will be asked to step down from your position." Both, in fact, did happen. The pastor addressed the key person generating the triangles most directly and in an appropriate way. The facts of the situation,

---

[3] Chapter 6 goes into ideal relationships more fully.

when brought out into the open, showed the leadership what next steps were needed. Had Pastor E become emotionally reactive to the situation and unable to think clearly about how to handle this misconduct, he very well might have become symptomatic, unable to function. He probably would have lost his position.

4. Encourage and incubate creativity in the group.

An unsure leader can contribute to getting any group stuck in more than one way. One of the most frequent is in stifling the flow of creative ideas. Since a group needs innovative thinking in order to survive and thrive, a high functioning leader needs to be able to nurture its creativity. If, as a reaction to his or her own unsureness, all the ideas have to come from him or her, the leader is in an overfunctioning position. This leads to underfunctioning of the group (and burnout in the leader). Their best thinking will be shut down or people will fear advancing their ideas.

In similar fashion, if someone has a good idea and immature members of the group come to the unsure leader, talking down the idea, the unsure leader will usually listen to the immaturity, squelching the good idea. Again, nothing ever gets done. And people are afraid to think creatively. They know their ideas will come to nought. The group can't move out of idle. Everyone, including the leader, will wonder why.

A better-functioning leader does not have to have all the ideas and, more than that, will be as enthusiastic for good ideas of others as for his or her own. In the same way, when the immaturity tries to negate the solid ideas and directions brought up for discussion, the more sure leader knows how to calm the anxiety and support solid ideas of others that are worth trying. If only some of the ideas come from the leader, but some or many from the group, the group will take off. They will have much more energy for implementing their own ideas than anyone thought possible. This is because they are out of the underfunctioning posture that was induced by the leader's overfunctioning or, in other cases, by the immaturity being in control.

5. Understand immaturity but don't side with it.

Some people in the group are more mature than others. The more emotionally mature people of the group are its strength. They are more likely to be candidates for leadership positions and produce solid thinking. That is, they more often have ideas that are well thought-through and based on logic and the realities of situations rather than on emotions. They will conduct themselves in ways that are more useful to the group and to themselves than the more immature members. They are a calming, thinking influence.

Immature people do have a place at the table, however. They may require more time from the leader, in simply connecting with them, and occasionally to drain off anxiety. But, they are understood as a valid part of the human spectrum and respected and related to from an equal posture. They can be members of the wider group, as participants, making worthwhile contributions. If they get in leadership positions, however, there may be trouble. It is necessary to be realistic about peoples' maturity levels, not expecting from them what is not possible.

Even the most solid members of the group, when under a load of anxiety, can show immaturity at times of stress. Under enough anxiety, the automatic fight or flight responses affect all of us. However, more mature people get less anxious and stay anxious for shorter periods. They often know what is needed to effectively manage the emotional side of self. They can get back to "calm" faster.

When anxiety is running high, the leader of the leaders needs to keep as calm and objective as possible, focusing on managing self, bringing as much logic to bear as possible, representing the best thinking of self. *Simply getting into the observing position can greatly assist in managing self during those stressful times.*

6. Bowen theory is for living, not for preaching.

Many people, with no training or expertise get excited about the ideas in Bowen family systems theory and try to write, teach or preach about it too early. While some simple facts, (such as the importance of the idea of cutoff, for example) may lend themselves to this, in general, most people who jump into explaining complexities while still learning, do poorly. In the process, they represent theory inaccurately. When difficult questions arise, they are lost. If they would stick to gaining a personal understanding of the ideas for a few years, simply striving to live them out, they would do much better. Teaching these ideas, at best, comes far down the line.

7. Defining what you are and are not willing to do.

Many clergy people seem to be born overfunctioners. This puts them at risk for doing what others need to be doing. Many clergy people do, literally, everything. If instead, they learn to define for themselves, what they can and cannot do, they can also communicate this to the group. People understand that we all have limits. What they don't understand is limits that are not explained to them. Some common boundary incursions include those on family time, days off, hours or weeks worked, phone call misuse, popping in the clergy residence unannounced (especially when the manse or parsonage is nearby) and using clergy for jobs not properly theirs (such as being the church secretary). All of this can be managed if it is simply defined in one's head and stated to others at the appropriate times and places. The sooner this happens in one's tenure, the better. Some defining of self is best done even in the call negotiation stage. After a pattern gets established, it is more difficult to change.

8. Making contact with anxious "problem" people.

In a congregation there are always immature anxious "problem" people, just as in a family. Just as we head *towards* them in our families, we do well to do the same in the congregation. They will be less a problem if leaders relate to them out of logic and intellect, unafraid of the anxiety and not taking it on. Sometimes they are really not trying to cause trouble, but simply trying to connect inappropriately. Sometimes they are simply from an anxious system, or going through an anxious time. The group can unload anxiety on individuals by overfocusing on them, unwittingly pressing them into the role of "anxiety carrier" or "problem person." It is up to the leader to get a different relationship with such a person, one that is more open and less anxious. Often he or she will respond to this kind of a relationship by being less anxious and less of a problem. They may take a bit of time but they are worth it. If one can be separate, open, and equal with them, one can be with anyone. When we start to observe them, considering them not a problem, but a great training ground (as they are in our families, too) for relationship skills, they are more of a performance challenge than a "problem." When this happens, the whole group benefits.

When one man distanced himself from Pastor J, because of perceived slights, he stopped attending church and then emitted negative remarks about the pastor around the congregation. He would not respond to invitations for time in the office. One day the pastor took a chance and called, saying he was in the neighborhood. "Would it be okay if I stopped in?" he asked. It was and he did. This connection was received so well that the parishioner shared a great deal of personal history in a conversation that continued for hours. The negative jabs as well as the distance were over and he resumed his regular attendance at church.

9. Manage emotional process in meetings.

All too often, in board or committee meetings, important meetings are held in the evening. People are already tired at that time of the day, so there is one strike for elevated emotional process. Further, the normal stimulative effect of people getting together operates. Strike two. The sometime perplexing issues that must be addressed provide strike three. Under those circumstances, most meetings and conversations can be frustrating. When someone doesn't agree with someone else's ideas, the anxiety rises. Repeat this process several times in one meeting and the tension level can be such that no one's brain is operating reliably. All useful cerebral activity is wiped out by the brains' emotional centers of those present.

Actually, people go to a meeting to think through to solutions, to get something accomplished. If one were to devise the least productive way to get results, the above paragraph would be the perfect way to do it. In a high anxiety setting, the logical, thinking brain doesn't work very well. There are two ways this can be addressed:

- When anxiety rises, the leader works harder than usual *to be the calm logic* at the table. Speaking after others have been heard, he or she is firm, defining self clearly and logically. Where the leader is not sure of the way to go, one can honestly say that, and ask for more time for the issue to simmer in people's thinking. The calm thoughtfulness of the leader is "catching" by the rest of the group and has a wonderful effect.

- Meetings can be structured so that group emotional process (the anxiety that circulates around systems) does not resonate and escalate. *If people talk to the chair and not to each other,* group emotional process (where emotions escalate to the point of no thinking), groupthink (where one dominant voice or viewpoint prevails to the exclusion of all others) and other forms of emotionality in group form will not be as likely. People get their work done and get home at a reasonable hour.

Extraordinary Leadership Seminars are structured in this manner. After a short period of adjustment to the process, many clergy, seeing the value, have tried the same structure in their groups. They give back very positive feedback on their experiments.

Rev. L predicted there was a good chance that a certain committee meeting would be intense, since the interlocking triangles on both sides of a certain issue had begun to take shape. She met with the chair person ahead of time, coaching her to try something new and field all the discussion, letting all comments come to her as chair. At the outset, the pastor said a few words about making the meeting into a thoughtful process rather than based on emotion, explaining that they needed to resolve the issue and the brains present would function better under those circumstances. Then the chair took charge. The meeting went better than usual. It stayed fairly calm and thoughtful. The issue was resolved. Later, people who were present asked if they could run other meetings in the same manner.

10. Who are we working on, the group or self?

Many teachers of Bowen theory seem to think that family systems theory is about changing or managing the group in some way. It is true that family systems theory does teach us a great deal about group emotional behavior. It is also accurate that groups change for the better when leaders work on themselves. But, *the primary effort goes to self and learning to relate better—not to changing the group.* A higher functioning leader will automatically spawn a higher functioning (and even grateful) group. *As the leader goes to higher levels of functioning, the group comes up to meet him or her.*

The best leaders have the best family relationships

There are several reasons why becoming a better leader entails working on oneself in one's family relationship system.

1. Early on, *Bowen found that the therapists he was training who took the ideas back into their own families and worked on themselves there, made superior progress to those who did not.*[4] We all have counterproductive automatic patterns of behaving that get triggered from time to time. Most originated in childhood in the family

---

[4] Bowen, M, *Family Therapy in Clinical Practice*, Aronson, New York, 1978, p. 533.

triangles. The most effective way of being freed of these maladaptive patterns is to work on them in our original families If we are trying to change a pattern that does not serve well, there is no substitute for working on it in the emotional field where it developed. That is hard work, but still not as hard as working in one's present nuclear family, where one lives. Yet it is extremely effective.

2. *If immature ways of relating—and we all have them—are present they will create anxiety in the family system.* No one is immune to creating this kind of anxiety and passing it on to the family. In the same way, we all take on anxiety from the family. It circulates throughout all the individuals in a family and then back again. That is part of the definition of an emotional system. If one works toward getting better family relationships in his or her original family, some of this anxiety will be resolved for good. Then there is simply less to carry around. There is less to transmit to the organization.

3. *The leader who is working on improving self in family relationships is a different—and better—kind of leader.* He or she is more accessible, more equal, more open. Some of the people in the family have a way of seeing us as not so special after all, often a needed equalizing phenomenon. Many who work on getting in touch with their generations talk of the grounding effect this had on them. Others, single and somewhat lonely, talk of how consoling and calming it is to have previously distant family "there" for them.

4. *We can "grow" more maturity in any arena of life. But the original family is the most efficient place to do it.* Even if most of the family is gone, there are almost always some surviving branches where the emotional process of the family is alive and well. If no one can be located, a friendship system can be a fair substitute in which to do the needed relationship work.

So, congregations, while they are not families, have many of the same characteristics. We can learn best about emotional processes in our own families. We can change ourselves there the most efficiently. And we all have areas of ourselves that need work.

Thinking It Over

As one observes and manages one's own anxiety, relationship functioning improves. If leadership relationships improve, there is less anxiety in the congregation. Relationships improve congregation-wide. This frees energy of the group to do its mission.

Knowledge of emotional systems enables one to see and understand the anxiety behind relationship patterns. Thus, one is a little more "out" of the emotional system. It enables one to push up functioning in all areas. In short, the new lens shows how to lead.

Real Live Research

1. How is a congregation like a family?

2. How is it not like a family?

3. What does it take to develop an emotional system?

4. How does working on self in one's family help a leader?

5. How are "problem people" important—in the scheme of things—and to one's own efforts to "step up"?

6. Can you think of patterns in your congregation/organization presently that belie anxiety?

7. Why is being a little "out" of the emotional field of the congregation/organization useful for a leader?

8. Can you think of areas where you might define yourself to your group better?

9. Are you an overfunctioner in your group? How hard is being an equal for you?

10. Do you see ways you might step down from that lofty position?

11. What is a "virtual family"?

12. How can a leader of a large congregation keep contact with the entire unit, including its "virtual families"?

3

How Groups Shape Individuals

The emotional process of groups tends to press people into a position. It may be favorable, assisting them in doing their best for self and for the organization. Or, the emotional slot into which an individual is compressed, may be an anxious one, and, thus, not as favorable. He or she may find that there is no way to function in it. There may be too much anxiety for the person to be able to do a good job. In the best of situations, a group, with a leader thinking systems, can bring out the best in a person so that he or she can develop more positive qualities and do well for the group, with a minimum of anxiety.

How groups shape individuals in organizations will make more sense if we first see how this works out in the family.

Family immaturity, projected

It is clear that our family experience during our young, dependent years shapes and sculpts who we become to a considerable degree. While many of the details of this process are known, there is much still to be learned.

When Bowen began his work, so-called "schizophrenogenic" mothers were still being talked about in research literature and at scientific gatherings. In those days, it was thought that something the mother was doing to the child was "causing" the child's illness. While Bowen didn't see it quite that way, he did, in the very beginning, study mother-child pairs. He soon realized, that though the mother was an extremely important player, the whole family was involved. It was an emotional unit, including the father and all the siblings—even the child played a primary role!

The emotions circuited around the whole group. Sometimes most of the immaturity seemed to end up in one person. It appeared to be "projected" on to that one. Therefore, he called that phenomenon the "family projection process." It showed why different siblings in the same family were different in their ability to adapt and to adjust to whatever they needed to. Some were just better at managing the complexity of living—creating a better life course—than others.

Family projection process

The projected-on children do less well. They are over-focused—anxiously, or even over-positively. This anxiety may take several forms. It may be simply a worried focus, showing a lack of confidence in the person. It may be expressed as oppositional, where every idea the person has, or every contribution he or she tries to make, is thwarted. It may be an over positive expectation that no one could live up to. In either case, the person ends up with more "chronic anxiety," and less maturity. Their nervous systems operate differently as a result. No one does well when anxious. So they develop symptoms of one kind or another, either physical, mental/emotional, or social. They are more "fused" (linked emotionally, dependent on, a part of) to their parents, taking on more of the family immaturity.

There are many factors that affect the family projection process. Some would be:

- Anxiety level of the family at the time of the birth of the child, or at important times later on—events taking place in the extended family during and around the time of birth and in early childhood such as business changes, moves, or cutoffs,

- Nodal events such as deaths or births that affect the family triangles, setting off anxious intensity in the nuclear or extended families,

- Sibling position—a particular family may tend to focus more on the oldest male, or the only female, for example,

- Maturity level of the parents and unresolved anxiety in their relationship,

- Functional positions of parents and siblings in the parents' families,

- An only child,

- Any "difference," such as a handicapped child or one born wih an illness or disorder.

Any, several, or all of these factors can combine in any one family to shape the process itself.

Other children, though in the same family, with less projection, or focus, do better. They take on less of the family anxiety and immaturity and thus are freer to develop in a way that enables them to explore, relate to and learn from the world around them. They are less fused with their parents.

In this way, it is possible, even usual, that children in the same family show very different life courses. The family projection process shows why it is possible for children in the same family to turn out so differently.[1]

Multigenerational transmission process

The generations of the family play into who each of us becomes. They help to shape attitudes, beliefs, and whether a

---

[1] See Gilbert, R., *Connecting With Our Children,* Wiley, New York, 1999, for a fuller discussion of projection to a child, especially pp. 1-114.

given nuclear family is on a downward spiral, heading to more immaturity, or on the upswing, going towards better levels of maturity. The effects of major events such as migration, persecution, holocaust and famines, or economic reversals may be felt through many generations.

Sibling position in the family constellation

In addition, Dr. Walter Toman, working in Europe, found by careful and voluminous research, that the very order and gender mix people fall into in their families have an influence on their personalities, preferences, professions, and relationships. Even that of their parents influences their own, to a degree.[2]

For example, a sister of sisters may always "need" some time with her women friends. Similarly, a brother of brothers can experience the "need" for time with his male friends. And if their spouses understand that, all will be smoother. On the other hand, sisters of brothers and brothers of sisters are less likely to need time with their own gender. They are just as happy to spend time with their spouses.

Leadership is influenced by sibling position too. Oldest or only children in a family are more apt to become leaders in later life. It is said that a large percentage of the people on the front of Time Magazine are "oldests" or "onlies."

Youngest children tend to know how to make people laugh. They are good "followers" or team members.

Middle children are known for their relationship skills and for their peacemaking abilities.

Toman's research made it possible for him to describe statistically typical "portraits" for all the eleven positions in the family. They are: oldest brother of brothers, youngest brother of brothers, oldest brother of sisters, youngest brother of sisters, oldest sister of sisters, youngest sister of sisters, oldest sister of

---

[2] Toman, W., *Family Constellation,* Springer, New York, 1961.

brothers, youngest sister of brothers, middle children, twins and only children, both male and female.[3]

When Bowen learned of Toman's work, he instantly recognized that it rounded out family systems theory and was actually needed as a separate concept in it. That concept would become known as "sibling position."

He also saw that sibling position was not the whole story, as did Toman himself. Other emotional forces in the family were important modifiers. Toman thought that, while the portraits were quite accurate statistically, in any individual case they might or might not hold. He would always add the caveat, ". . . all things being equal."

Of course all things are never equal, and so the portraits rarely hold 100 percent for any individual case. Some statements are accurate and some are not. Very often, however, people read the portraits and exclaim, "How can someone who has never met me know me so well?" But, how do we account for the research that doesn't fit? And how does it happen that some people seem to fit an entirely different portrait better than their own?

When taken together with the rest of Bowen theory, especially the family projection process, we can usually make sense of the process in a given family. For example, an oldest, because of an anxious focus, may be unable to take the lead among siblings. The family will often look to the next in line to act as an "oldest."

Functional positions in our families.

The three concepts, family projection process, multigenerational transmission process, and sibling position, together, and acting as forces on each of us, explain a great deal of how family sculpting of offspring takes place. They enlighten

---

[3] For a summary of these positions, see Gilbert, R., *Extraordinary Relationships,* Wiley and Sons, New York, 1992, Appendix III or Gilbert, R., *The Eight Concepts of Bowen Theory,* Leading Systems Press, Basye, VA 2004, p. 85.

us on many of the mysteries of individual personality, showing us much about how we become who we are.

They go a long way to help us understand the roles we played in our families. Depending on how these three factors— sibling position, family projection process, and multigenerational transmission process—play out, then, we take on one or several "functional positions" in our families. In general, those positions stay with us through life. They form and forecast the particular persons we ultimately become.[4]

If one looked at the family story as a play in several acts, each character in the family would have a specific role. How the family constellation and projection process plays out for each of us is unique. In many families, one would be "the star" with the others playing supporting roles. In others, the play would look like more of a team effort towards various goals, but all the players' roles would be different. None of this, of course is planned by the family. Rather, it is automatic—outside the awareness of the family unit.

Most of us, however, as adults, can figure out what our roles in our families were. Most of us, with very little reflection, are able to fill in the blank "In my family, I was the one who_____."

Here are a few of the positions people often tell about:

1. The "good" one

He or she may be "needed" by the family who is worn out by a "rebel." These people are overfunctioners who try very hard to please those around them—doing for them, and anticipating their every need. They become uncomfortable if they perceive that they are not pleasing someone. Usually it is not a problem—they are good at accommodating. This effort wears them out from time to time, but generally they receive enough kudos back from their systems (family, then school, then work) to give them

---

[4] Gilbert, R.,, *Extraordinary Relationships,* op. cit., new edition in preparation.

energy. They may become over- or underfunctioners as adults, or alternate between the two.

2. The "rebel"

The rebel is in conflict with the world. Sometimes this person is playing out the parents' pattern of conflict, either in their marriage or in their generations. Rebels often suffer from inconsistent, or lack of, discipline. One rebel was related to by her mother as if she (the daughter) were the mother's older sister. (That relationship had been extremely conflicted.) The daughter turned out to have many of her aunt's personality characteristics. She and her mother continued the conflict over time.

Other rebels are responding to the unresolved anxiety in a parental triangle, where one parent, trying to define limits, would be undermined by the other, who, feeling sorry for the child, automatically opposes the first. This seems to be an intolerable situation for the youngster, who takes his or her anxiety out in angry, unwise and impulsive behavior.

Rebels can have, if they can tame their reactivity, a great ability to think for themselves. The rebel's preferred pattern in adult life is that of conflict.

3. The "sick one"

This one is usually playing out an intense, anxious child focus in the original family. The symptoms may be physical, mental/emotional, or social. He or she absorbed an inordinate share of the family anxiety/immaturity, resulting in symptoms. He or she may be in the unlucky sibling position (such as a middle child the author saw, where the parent's middle sister had been severely disabled) of a parent's sibling who was ill, physically, mentally or emotionally. The parent worries constantly that the child will turn out like his or her dysfunctional sibling. The projection process ensures fulfillment of the prophecy. The person grows up feeling dependent, and "unable." The common adult relationship pattern here is underfunctioning.

4. The "caretaker"

This functional position usually happens when one or both parents are incapacitated or unavailable. When the mother is absent or ill, often an older child is enlisted to care for younger siblings. Sometimes he or she must take care of the parent, too. Positive traits of the caretaker include skills in nurturing, helping others and creating a warm home atmosphere. A person in this position said, "I was glad my mother 'gave' me my younger sister. I wanted someone to love me since my mother was not there much." A downside of the caretaker can be over-responsibility. They can have a problem in being equals with other people and may tend to dominate. The favorite relationship pattern here is overfunctioning.

5. The "family therapist"

These people are "asked," in the family triangles, to solve the parental problem. They are relied on, asked advice, and sometimes they are inappropriately told intimate information about the parents' relationship. Sometimes, especially in cutoff or divorce they are expected to be messengers between the parents. Assets include a savvy about nuances of triangles and other aspects of relationships that escape others. They are sensitive and interested in people's problems. But, going through life trying to have all the answers and solving other people's problems can be tiring, and is not always appropriate. Sometimes people resent them as intrusive or too analytical. Their adult relationship pattern, of course, is that of overfunctioning.

6. The "star"

This person, often an only or oldest child, is looked to for high achievement in one or several fields of endeavor—it might be academics, athletics, music or art. He or she is supported in many ways by the family and so the person is greatly favored. The family rallies to their causes. As adults, they may be highly valued for various qualities they developed in their functional position. For example, "smart ones" can ultimately become an asset to any work group because of their knowledge and expertise. "Athletic ones" may be great team players in a work situation. If they keep on in their sport, they may have great physical health.

Unfortunately, in adult life they may be at a loss as to how to operate without all the support they have come to expect, though the world may bring them more than their share of it. They seem to attract it. If they haven't burned out in their field as children, they will often overfunction at work and for this they are esteemed and applauded. Personal relationships, though, may be difficult. Thus they over- and underfunction in relationships by turns.

7. The "comic"

These people are assets to the fortunate families who nurture his or her abilities, for the relief of anxiety they bring. Bowen, in talking of losses in a family, noted *"there are emotional losses, such as the absence of a light-hearted person who can lighten the mood in a family. A group that changes from light-hearted laughter to seriousness becomes a different kind of organism."*[5] Stephen Colbert[6] told, on a televised interview, of his years of efforts, after the early death of his father, to cheer up his mother. Most often the comic is the youngest in his or her family of origin. The assets of this position include: being liked by groups, an ability to diffuse anxiety, and an ability to see the bigger picture. The downside of the "comic" would be tendency to laugh off issues that might deserve serious thinking or action engagement. If youngests, they may be prone to underfunctioning.

8. The favored child

This position carries with it a natural aura of congeniality and is endowed with the positive regard and blessings of the family.

---

[5] Bowen, M., *Family Therapy, op. cit.* p. 325.
[6] Of the *Colbert Report*, on *Comedy Central*, interviewed *on Sixty Minutes*, August, 2006.

Later, as an adult, the person carries these gifts into any group. He or she is well-liked throughout life. If these people go into positions of clergy leadership, they become, for example, the "beloved pastor." Often they are at a loss to understand why everyone treats them so well. The downside is that their systems are ridden with one conflict after another. In the midst of the intensities, no one points a finger at this leader, though. Only if they start to think systems can they begin to see that they may actually be making a contribution to the difficulties the system is experiencing. Their tendency to be a little distant in relationships usually becomes apparent with observation. When they see that and engage a little more directly with the intensity and immaturity of the group, the system responds with positive energy. In relationships, their adult distance posture may have to be addressed on an ongoing basis.

Such are the variations found among family functional positions—and the importance of them to families! We carry with us through life the personality shaping of our functional positions. It includes sibling position and that of parents, but is more than that. It includes all the influences of the family maturity/immaturity balance—the fusions—and the effect of anxiety over critical periods upon the family, as well as how the immaturity is going through the generations, that somehow encouraged each of us into our unique spot in the family unit.

Given the human capacity for repetition, and how ingrained we all are into our positions, understanding what part one's functional position plays in the development of who we are becomes extremely important. *In fact, there will be little chance of surpassing their limiting aspects without understanding them as completely as possible.* Functional positions are not deterministic. People can profitably gain more flexibility, by working toward greater maturity, lessening their influence.

As we've seen, any functional position carries with it both assets and benefits. Each also has its weaknesses. The goal, of course, is to preserve the natural strengths conferred upon one by one's position while finding a way to go beyond its constraints. Understanding something about functional positions and all the various ways one is still automatically operating out of them can be most useful. At the same time, it is helpful to understand one's parents' position, since each parent is an important imprint upon every individual, profoundly affecting family interactions. It will be helpful to get outside of oneself as much as possible and observe one's behavior closely for automatic responses that were developed in early years but may now be inappropriate. Small, day-to-day behaviors are as revealing as any. Pushing against the limiting aspects derived from one's emotional systems, however, tends to heighten the favors bestowed by one's functional position in both individual and interpersonal functioning. It also lessens the disadvantages these positions leave us with.

For example, Mr. S had a life-long problem of excessive dependence on other people (expecting everyone to take care of him). His wife complained that he, by his passive stance, often pushed her into a dominant position. When he saw how this tendency stemmed from his sibling position as a youngest and focused child in his family of origin, he began to rework his relationships with his brothers and sisters. Instead of expecting them to do things for him and otherwise take responsibility in the relationships, he began to act more like a responsible self. For example, he began to initiate contact with each of them more often. He then worked on seeing himself as an equal with each of them. After that, he worked toward feeling equal in their presence. He made similar efforts in relationships with colleagues at work. This was a gradual process that actually took place over several years. Since his wife was not used to having an equal self as a partner, there were some conflictual reactions from her in the beginning. When he could remember to not react back, but stay in logical contact with her, these reactions were short-lived. As his work progressed, he noticed his wife's complaints about him diminishing. Over time their relationship functioned better and better. It was more satisfying to each.

Experiments with behaving differently can begin with questions such as "How would it look and feel to do differently even small behaviors that are derived from my family functional position?" Rehearsing them in one's head before trying them out in the system can be useful. For example, Dr. M became aware that her frequent confrontations with her oldest son had everything to do with the fact that she and her son were both oldests. As such, both liked to assert rather than listen, both liked to tell people what to do and both sought to have the last word in conversations. This realization helped her to make a shift in relating to him. If she continued in her bold, frontal "oldest" style in her relating to him, she began to understand that he would probably turn out to be either completely compliant or angry and rebellious. She needed to find a way to allow and encourage his being a self in the relationship while she continued to be a self—not putting herself into the adaptive, shut down or underfunctioning position. Managing herself differently, she was able to listen more to what he had to say. She acknowledged his assertions, accepted the "oldest" responsible side of him and yielded more responsibility over to him. She became a different type of parent to him. Their relationship worked much better.

Of inestimable value to her in this effort was the work she did on herself in her family of origin. She rethought her relationships with her siblings. As she began to see them more as equals and less as "little" brothers and sisters, those relationships became friendships. Instead of always telling or advising them, she sometimes asked their opinions. More of the time she found a way to simply be there with them. Her relationship with her son lost its angry, confrontational mode and he blossomed into a natural leader. Mother and son gained genuine respect for one another.

With practice in relating to one's actual sibling(s) differently, with behaviors and goals in mind, well-set neural patterns gradually give way. First attempts at changing any behavior are always awkward, but with patience comes progress. Interestingly, the gains are seen best in retrospect. In the middle of working on self one may not see a lot of progress. It is in looking back that a totally different and better quality of life is most apparent.

Family functional positions, derived from the patterned functioning within the family triangles, illustrate once more the staying power of early family relationship patterns, in each of us and in our systems. *But they are not set in stone. They are merely starting points for adults who want to work on becoming all they can be.* When we start to see them in ourselves, possibilities open that will help plot a course toward transcending their limitations while preserving their strengths, an important step in the process of becoming a high level leader.

Congregational positions

Congregations, of course, are an aggregation of many different personalities, formed from the families in which they were shaped. We are who we are. We were shaped into that person over many years of emotional connection in a group. And, we take that with us wherever we go. All of this explains a large part of the difficulty in understanding the complexity of organizations.

If that were not enough, there is more. *The organization itself, because it is an emotional system, will try to press its members into functional positions just as does a family.* And, it does this in a manner similar to the family—just by how it sees people, what it asks of them, and out of its own emotional needs. Like the family, it is not aware of this process. And it certainly is not intentional about it. It just occurs, over time.

For example, in any group, there are those who have seniority. They have been there longer than anyone else. Often, they behave like oldest children in a family. They may assume ownership of the group. And, often, emotionally speaking, they do own it. Then, there is the "last to come" phenomenon of newcomers. Those people may be treated as if they are youngests. They may be pushed around as if they are less competent or knowledgeable.

Leaders will often be oldest children in their families. They may even come from a long line of "oldests" in their generations. They may be so sure in that functional position that others regularly fall in line with them. If a "youngest" (in his or her family) somehow becomes the leader, he or she may often seem to be unsure, losing confidence, asking for advice, not knowing what to do. Who does he or she ask? The oldests, of course!

Organizational projection process

Groups can also focus on one of their members anxiously, just as parents do. The focus, with its transfer of anxiety, can make it impossible for that one to function.   Similarly, a position within the organization can be the object of focus. One head nurse told the story of taking a position that was steeped in a history of such intense focus that no one had been able to stay there long. The job had seen many good people come and go. She herself was not able to last long. She received the same intense focus, making it impossible for her to do her work.

An organization, by a projection process similar to that in a family that "does in" a child, can transmit anxiety to anyone in a given position. Under those conditions, it becomes very difficult for anyone to function.

Leadership guidelines

What directions can a leader take, where a group seems to be pressing people into unwelcome molds?

- Knowledge of *sibling positions*, people's maturity levels and functional positions can be revealing in untangling the threads of what is going on. Over time, one can become quite adept in seeing the process at work.

- Understanding *who came when* (longevity) in the congregation is important.

- The *leader may be one of the "last to come."* In that case, *a research posture,* learning all one can from those who have been there longer can be invaluable. It can help one gain knowledge about the organization and how it operates. Simply observing is extremely calming, making logical thought possible.

- The leader may need, from time to time, to *lighten up the atmosphere with humor* that gives a bigger picture, lessening the intensity, if people or their positions are receiving anxious overfocus.

- The *leader's showing confidence in the overfocused person* can be a life line to the person in that position, not only in how the person functions, but also on giving cues to the group, indicating a higher road. *It is actually doing the relationships well that is useful, not telling the group how to do it.*

Negative focus on the leader

If the triangles start to focus negatively on the leader of the organization, it can become difficult for him or her to operate. Meeting with the anxious angles of triangles can help to dissipate such anxiety if the leader makes an effort not to take on the anxiety. If criticisms are warranted, there is no use in denying them. It is better to admit where one needs to focus more effort and then get on with making the necessary changes in self. Making needed changes in the family relationships as a primary effort will greatly help. But if the group is acting more out of anxiety than factual difficulty of the leader, the leader can:

- Remember that *being different draws focus. The leading position is unique, so focus will occur from time to time. It may be positive or negative.* It should be expected, as just part of the job description.

- *Refuse to take on the anxiety*, but stay connected with the anxious individuals.

- *Do some research*, if necessary, to uncover the facts. Think according to the facts and logic of the situation. Represent that thinking to the group.

- *Focus on mission, goals, and guiding principles.*
  Articulating them to the group is useful, if they have been
  worked out. If not, that may be part of the problem and
  ⬤ing to work on defining them may be exactly what the
  group needs. Direction, the sureness of reliance on
  principles, appropriately addressing issues, and focus on
  tasks, are all the marks of a high level leader.

Becoming a better leader, for most of us, involves
understanding group emotional process and knowing effective
ways of addressing it. Extraordinary Leadership may mean
dropping some familiar postures. This not an easy task but it is
one that carries with it great rewards into the future.

Thinking It Over

The mix of ages and gender together with the influence of the
family projection process and the multigenerational process
work in combination to create the functional positions we grew
up in. They play a huge part in making us who we are.
Understanding these influences becomes a starting point for the
work of managing and modifying their weaknesses, while
emphasizing their advantages. Organizations can press people
into functional positions just as families do. Family systems
theory shows the way out.

Real Life Research

1. Fill in the blank; "In my family I was the one
    who_____."

2. What family influences or events do you think worked, along with sibling position tendencies toward that outcome? Do you see it in your life today?

3. What were functional positions of your parents?

4. Who received the most focus in your sibling group? Who, the least?

5. What strengths/weaknesses of your family position would you like to keep/modify?

6. Do you see congregation/organization members being influenced by their own family functional positions?

7. Is your organization pressing its members into functional positions of its own?

8. Do you need to play a role in modifying any of this?

9. What could you do?

10. Have you, as a leader, been the object of a negative focus from the group?

4

A Natural Systems View of Hierarchy

The phenomenon of hierarchy is ubiquitous among human groups. It is found in many other species as well. It is an important phenomenon for leaders to think about because like other relationship patterns based in the emotional centers of the brain, it is automatic, and probably a part of every group

Some of the work that has been done on the subject, both in other species and in the human, follows.[1] Since the emotional part of the human brain is so similar to that of other species, we can learn much about our own patterns by studying these systems. Often, too, a look at natural systems increases objectivity. The lens of family systems theory is of great importance to make sense of hierarchy.

Definitions

In living systems and in this chapter, hierarchy means a ranking of all the individuals within it from highest to lowest, according to social status. It is observed in many different

---

[1] This chapter was adapted from a paper of the same name by Roberta Gilbert, read at Georgetown Family Center's Conference on Organizations, April 23, 1995.

species. It is an emotional or instinctual organizational pattern and is probably present in all groups.

Social hierarchy in other species

Some of the best descriptions of hierarchical behavior—the relationship behaviors between individuals that lead to a hierarchical group formation in different species—were provided by Price and Sloman.[2]

In other species, they explain, winning and losing seems to be an integral part of group behavior and contributes to hierarchical group structure. Lorenz described *ritual agonistic behavior (RAB)* as a form of signaling between two individuals to create, readjust, or reinforce asymmetry of behavior resulting in an agreed-upon winner and loser. There is a need for recognized winners and losers in a group since a symmetrical behavioral relationship has a potential for escalating conflict and thus, the instability of the group. These "asymmetrical relationships" in a matrix form a social hierarchy.[3]

Dawkins refers to the yielding (submissive, subordinate) component of "RAB" as a "yielding subroutine." "Hardware" for this behavior was located in the "reptilian" brain by MacLean who, by ablating various portions of the brain, pinpointed areas that control specific functions.[4]

Schjelderup-Ebbe's "pecking order" in birds is well known.[5] It is a hierarchical arrangement where there is one bird that no others peck that can peck any of the others. The second bird in the hierarchy is pecked by only that one, does not peck the top one, but can peck all the others, and so on, down the line.

DeWaal has described hierarchy and the behaviors by which it is identified in his studies of chimpanzees at the Arnhem Zoo.

---

[2] Thanks to Stephanie Fererra for providing this paper to this author.
[3] Price, J.S., and Sloman, 1987 "Depression as Yielding Behavior: An Animal Model Based on Schjelderup-Ebbe's Pecking Order," *Ethology and Sociobioloby*, 8:855-98S.
[4] *Ibid.*
[5] *Ibid.* See extended quote on pp. 55-56.

He classified and compared 15 behavioral variables stemming from agonistic and competitive interactions. These included nine agonistic (aggressive) variables such as the "rapid oh-oh," non-vocal bluff, kissing and grooming. He also studied two behaviors not considered agonistic which he thought could be considered evidence of a pecking order or hierarchy in the group. He called these "self evident indisputable rights" such as "competition-space" (approach-retreat or avoidance) and "competition-social" (refraining from contact with a partner because another chimp takes up contact with that individual).[6] Triangles of this nature are often seen in descriptions of other species.

DeWaal also studied phenomena related to hierarchical reciprocity in three different primate species—chimpanzees, rhesus monkeys, and stumptail monkeys. He watched for interactions of revenge and found a complex picture characterized by different types and degrees of hierarchical behavior in different species. While the monkeys can not be relied upon to take revenge upon an individual of higher rank after an "agonistic intervention" (an aggressive behavior), chimpanzees have subtle and sometimes complex ways of retaliating against their superiors. There is, for example, "a democratic tendency in chimpanzee society." Individuals of lower status seem to try to influence the configuration at the top of the hierarchy. Middle-ranking individuals direct a disproportionate amount of their interventions at conflicts among individuals positioned above them. There is also considerable female involvement in status struggles among dominant males. In social interactions such as grooming, the monkeys show more asymmetry in these behaviors, and thus, a more rigid hierarchical society than did the chimpanzees, who tended to reciprocate more in grooming.[7]

---

[6] DeWaal, Frans and Luttrell, L, 1998 "Three Primate Species: Symmetrical Relationship Characteristics or Cognition?", *Ethology and Sociobiology*, 9:101-118.
[7] *Ibid.*

Hierarchy in the human species

Examples of human hierarchical organizations are plentiful. Some of the more prominent include businesses, religious organizations, and the military services. They are well-known human organizations built according to clear and explicit hierarchical lines. Other groups, such as the Mafia, could also be mentioned as examples of hierarchical organizations.

Religious organizations often have a leader at the top with other high level leaders just below. Local organizations with their own leaders and hierarchical arrangements are under these top leaders.

In military combat where direction must be decided quickly, there may not be time for the rational discussion needed for consensus that may be brought into play at other times. Thus, in this case the realistic need for hierarchy is evident.

Hierarchy among humans is a way to organize complex groups, whether implicitly or explicitly. It is probably present in every group and even in every relationship, to some degree. Like triangles, and other relationship patterns, it may more clearly be seen at times of higher anxiety in the group.

The cost and benefits of hierarchy

What price is paid for hierarchy? Price and Sloman suggest that when two animals engage in a fight for dominance, the losing animal shows signs of depression that reassure the winner that further fighting or discouragement are not necessary and that the loser is incapable of making a comeback. Schjelderup-Ebbe commented that:

". . . hens lead a more or less worry-free existence according to their position on the peck order." [A low-ranking hen was] very nervous because of the number of pecks she received. I had the impression that she tired herself out in a constant attempt to avoid punishment and to get enough food. [The high-ranking hen] who was never bothered by anybody, seemed to feel very well. . . it is possible to trace the order of despotism in the appearance of the birds. Those which are despots over many

thrive, become stout, look contented: those in the middle rank are usually normal: those which have nearly all the others over them are thin, restless, and often pine away. In the case of magpies and other birds which live in the same manner, we can correctly conclude which birds stand high on the pecking list and which low from the brightness of the plumage and the appearance of cleanliness. Those which stand low have rumpled, disordered plumage, often with dirt hanging to it, while the birds that have good social conditions have bright, sleek, beautiful and clean plumage. The birds which are dirty have little opportunity to clean themselves and keep themselves in order, partly because they are often chased immediately if they stand still, and partly because so much of their energy is used in obtaining food. "[8]

Similarly, Sapolsky's work with olive baboons pointed out the stressful nature of life at lower levels of the primate social hierarchy by measuring adrenocortical hormonal activity over time in individuals at different positions on the hierarchy. He was able to see striking differences in the levels of stress the animals lived with by the chronic differences in levels of adrenocortical hormones.[9]

Hierarchy in Bowen family systems theory

How can we account for hierarchical behavior from the perspective of Bowen theory? Bowen described a relationship posture called "the dysfunctional spouse" or "the adaptive posture," later referred to as overfunctioning/underfunctioning reciprocity where the underfunctioning person "gives up self" to the overfunctioner in the reciprocal relationship. *"This is the result when a significant amount of undifferentiation is absorbed in the adaptive posture of one spouse.*[10] The dominant one

---

[8] Price and Sloman, *op cit.*

[9] Sapolsky, R, *Stress, the Aging Brain and the Mechanisms of Neuron Death,*. Cambridge, MA, MIT Press, 1992.

[10] Differentiation is discussed in the next section. It can be roughly equated to immaturity.

assumes more and more responsibility for the twosome." [11] This relationship posture may be homologous to Lorenz's ritual asymmetrical behavior, with the *yielding subroutine of Dawkins strikingly similar to underfunctioning as described by Bowen.*

Bowen described the effects of underfunctioning, or the "adaptive" posture: "*The one who functions for long periods in the adaptive position gradually loses the ability to function and make decisions for self. At that point, it requires no more than a moderate increase in stress to trigger the adaptive one into dysfunction, which can be physical illness, emotional illness, or social illness, such as drinking, acting out, and irresponsible behavior.*" [12] This description by Bowen of a human relationship phenomenon would seem to be identical to descriptions of individuals at lower levels on hierarchies of other species.

In non-family emotional units, too, it is easy to see how a series of these posturings (overfunctioning/under-functioning reciprocities in relationships from the top to the bottom) can form a hierarchy. In this way, theoretically, the individual at the bottom of the hierarchy would be contributing self to each individual of higher rank in the system. The second individual from the bottom in rank would contribute self to everyone except the lowest one, but would be gaining some self from that one, and so on, up to the top. The individuals at the top of the hierarchy would be considered to be gaining the most self. The individuals at the bottom would be donating or giving up the most. There would be all gradations in between these two positions. Bowen described the adaptive or underfunctioning position as being at risk for physical or other symptoms. The one in a more dominant position does better, all things considered. That one is gaining some self from all the lower ranking members.

---

[11] Bowen, M, 1978, *Family Therapy in Clinical Practice,* Jason Aronson, p. 378.
[12] Bowen, *Family Theory,* ibid.

If hierarchy is so readily observed among species, it must be assumed that it is a useful part of all life. What is the function of hierarchy? In other natural systems, it seems to be a stabilizing force with the function of minimizing conflict in the group. No doubt hierarchical systems function for human organizations in the same way they do in other species, since the emotional brains and emotional, automatic functioning between humans and other species are so similar. As the underfunctioning individuals show more symptoms, they convey less threat to the overfunctioners, so conflict becomes unnecessary and in this way the group becomes more stable. But this stability comes at a dear price to some of the individuals. Their dysfunction means they can't contribute as much or as well to the group.

Like other characteristics of the emotional system such as triangles, conflict or distance, hierarchy can be considered neither good nor bad. Since humans are more like other species emotionally than they are different from them, they show emotional patterns similar to those of other species.

Individuals further up the social status ladder apparently are better off physiologically and seem to gain their advantage at the expense of those further down. And yet, even for those on the lower rungs of the hierarchy, the benefits of being a part of the group may yet compensate for physiologic and other consequences of status. That is, it may be better to survive with symptoms than not to stay in the group at all, which could mean an inability to survive.

If hierarchy is a result of emotional programming—the automatic group interaction behavior we share with other species—then, as with other automatic patterns, we might expect that when anxiety rises, hierarchical behavior would be more in evidence. When the group is relatively calm, hierarchical behavior would be less in evidence and individuals could treat each other more as equals, rank being less apparent and important. For example, an emotionally mature general in the heat of battle would be expected to tell the troops what to do— give orders. In peacetime, or away from the battle, in relationships with his peers, he might have a more egalitarian style in his relating with others.

Understanding systems as a guide

Systems thinking provides a way of thinking about the relationships of individuals in systems that goes beyond the more automatic reactive behavior of other species. Differentiation of self, in "broad terms similar to an emotional maturity scale" [13] yet different in some respects, defines the basic aspects of human functioning largely in relationship terms. The concept provides a way for any individual to think about managing self in a hierarchy, whether at the top or the bottom. For example, when the leaders of an organization are acting out of a more emotionally mature position, one might expect them, by thoughtful focus on self, to display an open and facilitative posture to all members of the group, regardless of status. Status would be less emphasized by these leaders than qualities needed by the group, such as the creative, productive, and self management potential of every member.

A leader using differentiation as a guide would keep the goals of the organization in focus without sacrificing the creativity, or the "self" of any individual member. Such a leader would encourage participation of all its members, bringing out the best in them and find ways to deal with less mature aspects of individuals and the group as they arose.

Likewise, members lower in the hierarchy, acting with differentiation as a guide, would seek to define self to other members at any level when necessary. This individual could openly communicate with anyone at any position if it were appropriate. Further, when hierarchical behavior becomes more prominent at times of increasing anxiety in an organization, it can be seen, by someone "thinking systems" for what it is, a manifestation of anxiety and managed accordingly rather than

---

[13] *Ibid*, p. 472. This is discussed more fully in Chapter 5.

allowing group emotional process such as hierarchy by itself to determine the group member's treatment or ultimate destiny.

Consideration of emotionally patterned reactions and interactions among individuals in a system can provide guidelines for people as they seek to survive current upheavals of organizations, such as shrinking denominations, the megachurch phenomenon, mergers, downsizing, and re-engineering.

Further, if hierarchy is a part of the emotional programming of the human, then attempts to reorganize organizations with the goal of doing away with hierarchy are probably destined for only limited success. In more emotionally mature or calm groups such a reorganization effort may modify hierarchical behaviors, to some extent, but it would be expected that an overt, or implicit hierarchy would in fact appear, in spite of best attempts to legislate it away. Because the vast majority of individuals possess a rather modest level of emotional maturity, to which relationship patterns are correlated, rarely are relationships free of the over/underfunctioning reciprocity entirely, and only a rare organization is relatively free of hierarchical organizing behavior.

The ideal organization

Presumably hierarchy, like other postures and patterns, would not exist in groups where every member was functioning at very high levels of emotional maturity.[14] The separation of selves would be so complete that there would be no need for the donating and lending that takes place in most relationships. People would interact as equals. Therefore, no member of the group would be "done in" by it. Anxiety levels would not differ as a function of being a member of the group. No one would develop symptoms, or do poorly simply by participating in relationships in that group. Different functions necessary to the survival of the group could be divided among its members without carrying any particular status. In this group it would be

---

[14] Described and explained in Chapter 6.

difficult for an observer to tell "leader" from "follower." Hierarchy, or status rank, would be a foreign concept although accomplishment could be recognized and valued by the group.

Thinking It Over

The phenomenon of hierarchy, or social status ranking in a group, is probably universal in many species and all human groups. It s seen as a derivative of over- and underfunctioning reciprocities in relationships. Hierarchical behavior can be seen more readily at times of heightened anxiety. Family systems theory shows a way of relating to all people in the group that is not emotionally or rank determined.

Real Life Research

1. Think of examples of hierarchies in families, in workplaces, in the government, in international relations.

2. What is the function of hierarchy in the wild?

3. Do you tend to over- or underfunction in relationships?

4. Does being in a leadership position tend to push you toward hierarchical behavior?

5. Does theory show a way of dealing with dominating people who tend to "take over?"

6. Can you keep your head thinking in the presence of a dominant person (loud, bossy or angry)?

7. What are triggers that tend to make you feel "less than" and then underfunction?

8. Who or what can trigger you into dominating a conversation, relationship or situation?

9. Have you ever seen a somewhat more egalitarian workplace? Describe what it was like.

10. How would the world be different if we all related to each other as equals?

PART II

THE SELF

—INDIVIDUALITY

"The individuality force is derived from the drive to be a productive, autonomous individual, as defined by self rather than the dictates of the group."

"The overall goal is . . . to rise up out of the emotional togetherness that binds us all."

Source for quotes on preceding page: Murray Bowen, *Family Therapy and Clinical Practice*, Aronson, 1978, pp. 277 and 371.

5

Human Variation

We have considered characteristics of emotional systems—togetherness and the many ways it plays out. There is, in addition, in all of us, a force opposite to the togetherness force called the individuality force. The individuality force resists the togetherness force (immaturity, or fusion, or unresolved emotional attachment) towards becoming all we can be—an individual who can cooperate in groups but is not dominated by its togetherness force.

The two forces combine in each individual differently—the more individuality, the less togetherness—to make for the infinitely fascinating variety we see among humans

Another most interesting fact is the difference in the ability people show in adapting in life—to set and fulfill goals, live out an orderly life course and make a contribution to their families and fellow citizens. Some seem to carry out a happy, useful life and become a resource to all who know them. Others, by contrast, have so many problems brewing all the time that they are usually on the brink, barely making it at all. Some live a long time, some don't. Some have good health, some don't. Some have satisfying and stable relationships. Others are hermits, angry rebels, or relationship nomads, seeming unable to attach in any meaningful way. Some delight in giving and serving others. Others make a living by thievery. Some benefit all of humanity. Some are terrorists.

Bowen theory describes this variation in human adaptation in some detail. The description helps us step up in functioning, sometimes just by simple exposure to the ideas contained in it. This most important concept is called *"the scale of differentiation of self."* It includes the idea of emotional maturity, but goes further. It literally shows us how to do better and better, the rest of our lives. It is not only concerned with removing symptoms. Also, there is no age limit for people to benefit. Differentiation becomes a lifelong project for most who take it on. Further, along with emotional, mental and social well-being, differentiation of self includes the physical aspects of life. It is a very broad idea indeed.

The scale of differentiation of self, which describes the individuality and togetherness balance of people, is a concept that describes all the differences in functioning of people, on a spectrum, from those who function best all the way down to those who barely scrape by.

There will probably never be a way to measure differentiation accurately, since it describes the whole of the life course. It is intended to convey an idea, not to measure people specifically and thus is more qualitative than quantitative—a way to think about human variation. Anyone's level on the scale can only be roughly estimated

The Scale

The scale of differentiation of self conceptualizes human functioning on a continuum from theoretical zero to theoretical 100—no one is that badly off or that well off. Rather, we are all somewhere in between those two absolutes.

The levels of functioning are similar to rungs of a ladder that go between two columns made up of emotions and intellect. At the bottom of the scale emotions and intellect are fused— intellectual functioning is driven by the emotions. In the middle, less so and further along, there is more and more choice about whether one is in emotions or intellect. At higher levels of functioning, the emotions and the intellect are more separate.

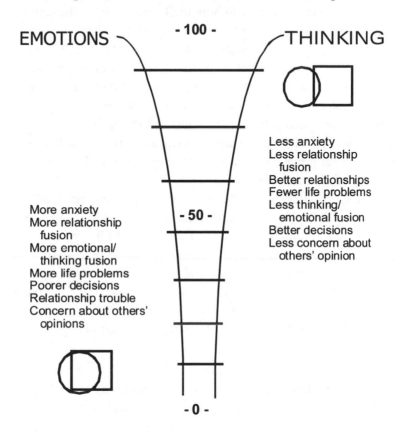

EMOTIONS — - 100 - THINKING

More anxiety
More relationship
  fusion
More emotional/
  thinking fusion
More life problems
Poorer decisions
Relationship trouble
Concern about others'
  opinions

- 50 -

Less anxiety
Less relationship
  fusion
Better relationships
Fewer life problems
Less thinking/
  emotional fusion
Better decisions
Less concern about
  others' opinion

- 0 -

Differentiation of Self Scale

We could not live without either emotions or intellect. The emotional—or automatic—part of man is almost identical to that of higher mammals. It is the instinctual reactive part of the brain. The automatic functions mean that we breathe, digest, and react to danger without the need to direct the processes, or think them through. *When these processes come into awareness, we refer to them as feelings.* The intellectual component makes us uniquely human, able to perform complex thinking, learning and understanding tasks, setting us apart from other species.

Dr. Paul MacLean, researching the brain at NIH at the same time Bowen was watching families, discovered that we have a "triune" brain.[1] Two of the layers, the lowest anatomically, are very similar to brains of other species. The *reptilian brain,* (or *"R complex"*) located in the lowest part of the brain, similar to that of reptiles, is responsible for survival physiology, reproduction and repetitive behaviors such as homing. The *limbic area* of the brain (*"paleomammalian"*), similar to that of other primates, makes possible parenting, audiovocal communication and play, for example.

Intellectually, we are different from all other species. Our *cerebral cortex,* the *"neomammalian"* is the distinguishing part of the human brain. It is tremendously developed in size and complexity compared to even our closest primate relatives. Because of its greater size, we are able to think ahead, think abstractly and symbolically, plan, empathize, speak, write, create works of art, and a tremendous number of other accomplishments that are uniquely human, at least in degree.

Lower levels of differentiation

Fusion of emotional and intellectual functioning at the lower end of the scale, means that, at those levels, much of behavior and thinking is emotionally driven. The emotions are so powerful that when a fusion of the two functions exists, intellectual functioning, not reliable in the presence of strong emotion, loses out. Since those at lower levels inherited a greater quantity of innate anxiety and reactivity from their interactions in the family system—the relationship fusions they grew up in—their intellectual processes will be affected by that. When

---

[1] MacLean, P., "A mind of three minds: Educating the triune brain." In *Education and the Brain, 1978,* The National Society for the Study of Education, University of Chicago Press, Chicago, p. 319 After Kerr, M *Family Evaluation,* Norton, New York, p. 35.

intellect is influenced, or made less effective by emotional forces, thinking is not logical or reliable. The finer abilities of the human, such as abstraction or the ability to see consequences of behavior, are lost. Thus, decision-making is impaired.

Poor decision-making means more life problems. Most of us bring on most of our life problems ourselves. And at the lower end of the scale, that tendency is multiplied by emotionally driven decision-making. Behavior is impulsive and not well thought-through. Life troubles abound.

There are also many relationship difficulties, partly because of the load of anxiety people at this level carry with them. Their greater anxiety leads to relationship patterns, as people tend to "take it out on each other," distance, dominate, underfunction, overfunction, or triangle.

People at this end of the scale live with an excessive amount of worry about what other people think. *Their whole world is one of relationships and emotional reactivity to them.*

There is no time or energy left to think about the wider world or other activities. Their contributions will be in terms of relationships—reacting to them positively or negatively. Much of the difficulty at the lower end of the scale can be attributed to the fusion of thinking and emotion. But the other type of fusion—relationship fusion—compounds the difficulties.

Fusions

In addition to the fusion of thinking and emotions, people at the lower end of the scale are characterized by their excessive unresolved emotional attachments, or relationship fusions, described earlier. In fact, *the emotional/intellectual fusion is probably derived or symptomatic of the relationship fusion.* These fusions, deep-rooted from years of experience in one's original family, are greatest at the lowest part of the scale. They derive from the family anxiety and focus that resulted in an excessive emotional attachment; first to parents, then to other important relationships. These attachments, if not resolved before leaving home, persist through life as an unrelenting tendency to attach to others to the same degree. This tendency is called *undifferentiation.* So, people at the lower end of the scale, if indeed they are able to leave home, go on to attach with someone with an equal amount of unresolved emotional attachment or undifferentiation. They are also apt to pass some of it on in their relationships with their children.

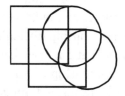

Family Fusions at Lower Levels

Going up the scale

Though we are stuck with the amount of undifferentiation we leave home with, it is possible to nudge it a little by effort, putting on a "new lens," and active, sustained coaching with someone who has been wearing that same lens a bit longer. That is the bad news. *The good news is that any movement at all up the scale means living a life that is all but unrecognizable from before.*

Higher levels on the scale

As we look at higher levels on the scale, we see all the challenging effects of undifferentiation lessening.

People higher on the scale have less ambient anxiety to carry around with them. This results in less reactive nervous systems. Because they were less the object of the projection process in their families, described earlier, they took on less anxiety in their original family years. In addition, they gain and lose less self in relationship fusions, which themselves are generators of anxiety. That means that the brain works better for decision-making as well as all kinds of complex intellectual functioning. Also, being less in the emotions/intellect fusion, the brain is freed of the intensity that holds it back from best functioning. Better decisions are possible. Because of that, there are fewer life problems. Relationships work better, the higher the position on the scale. And there is less unnecessary worry about what others think, whether one is loved or liked.

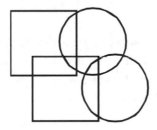

Family Fusions Higher on the Scale

Fusions of selves

Fusions of selves are at the basis of the differentiation/undifferentiation balance within each of us.

None of us had any say about which family we'd be born into. Some, born into a family at a lower level on the scale, grow up into intense fusions, where much self was lent and borrowed. These families demand that people think alike. They have little tolerance for difference. They demand much of their members. The family relationships themselves are emotionally demanding enough that there is little time or energy left over for any other pursuit. More undifferentiated families produce more undifferentiated people.

A little higher on the scale, the fusions are less. There is less togetherness force—along with all its demands—operating. People are freer to be a self. The family is less emotionally needy. They form a looser "togetherness." They are less demanding. There is more energy to pursue other interests than simply tending to relationships. They will form families whose members are higher functioning.

Still higher on the scale, relationship fusions are even less of a factor. Emotional attachment is more nearly resolved by the time people leave home. At high levels on the scale, relationships go well, often lasting from teenage years. People are less anxious, so they are subject to less symptoms of any kind. They make better decisions and so follow a more trouble-free life course.

Bowen thought that the great majority of people are 40 or below on this hypothetical scale. If one ever met a "50" one would be lucky. "75" on the scale would come along only once in every few hundred years.

Basic Self

Another way to understand the phenomenon of variation in human functioning is in terms of basic self and pseudoself (or functional self).

Basic self, the differentiated part of an individual, is the part that does not take part in relationship fusions. It is one's individuality. It has an intact boundary because it does not take on self from others or give up self to them. Basic self is guided by well thought-through principles. It knows what it believes and can stand there. It is not influenced by culture, relationships, or groupthink. For obvious reasons, it is often called "solid self."

The higher on the scale a person is, the larger basic self, the better thought-through are guiding principles and the smaller the pseudoself.

Pseudoself

Pseudoself is the part of us that engages in relationship fusions (undifferentiation, togetherness). For that reason, its boundaries are not intact, they are "leaky." It can, in overfunctioning, take on self from another person. In underfunctioning, it gives up self to the overfunctioner. The more undifferentiation, the larger is pseudo, or functional self.

Pseudoself is guided by reactivity, relationships, the culture, or education—whatever has not been well thought-through for the self. It can also be guided by the reactivity of the self. It is subject to groupthink.

The larger the pseudoself, the leakier the boundaries to taking on anxiety and self from others, and the smaller the basic self.

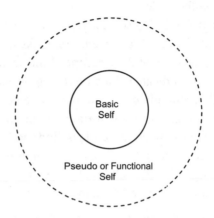

Basic and Pseudo or Functional Self [2]

High and low level leadership

High level leaders are higher on the scale of differentiation of self. They lead by well thought-through principles. They are not easily swayed by what others think if that does not jibe with their own principles. They are grounded in logic, the facts of situations, and thinking things through. They do not make snap decisions unless forced to by an emergency. In relationships, they stay out of conflict, distance, dominating or underfunctioning, and triangling. They tolerate human variation. They accept that not everyone functions as they do. They can make allowances for others. They do not react to someone not agreeing with them. They are high on the scale.

---

[2] This idea was put into a diagram in the 1980's by Kathleen Kerr.

Low level leadership is easily led by the group, especially the immature members who may be the loudest or the most intense. Their decisions are based more on relationship considerations than on principles. They have few principles, preferring to "go with the flow" or let others tell them what they think. They are especially subject to groupthink (domination by one, or a faction of a group process). They slip easily into relationship patterns. They are low on the scale.

Most of us probably fall somewhere between these two extremes. Theory, for mid-range leaders, makes a huge difference. Knowing about the concept of the scale of differentiation will indicate what a next step up for any given individual will be. Simply doing the work one needs to do, at work and in one's family makes for a different kind of leader. People who are working on these ideas find that people are attracted to them, wanting to know what and how they think about many things. This is high level leadership.

The best leaders work on being in contact:

- With their own families, nuclear and extended

- With congregational leaders, above and below their organizational status

- With congregational families

- With "virtual families"

This means one-to-one relationships, where each can talk about self and define self to the other, staying out of the relationship patterns.

Differentiation of self as a verb[3]

"What do we do to get to those attractive higher levels of functioning?"[4] The following are four of the efforts people make:

---

[3] From Kathleen Kerr.
[4] More detail on this subject is planned for the third text of the series.

1. Learn theory.

If we learn it we can use it. If we don't we can't. There are many opportunities for learning and they all need to be utilized if one is really serious. Theory is the best guide as one tries to grow more basic self

2. Manage anxiety.

One of the best ways to shore up one's boundaries (to be less permeable to anxiety) is to learn ways of relaxing in the face of anxiety. Relaxation techniques, logic, thinking (to activate the cerebral brain, inhibiting the emotional centers), exercise, prayer, and many others are useful to different people.

3. Gain more self in significant systems.

In one's original family, where the patterns were learned, they can be most effectively changed. But the work can continue in one's nuclear family and one's workplace. A coach is essential in these efforts.

4. Work on guiding principles.

Guiding principles, the hallmark of the high level self, always need more thinking time, more clarity—and more use!

Guiding principles are well thought-through, not adapted from family, education, or culture. Thus, it takes time and effort to gain them. They are tried out in the laboratory of life. Then they can be adopted.

Guiding principles are not set in stone. They can be revised if new data dictate that. Guiding principles are not held in a closed mindset (a fundamentalist attitude).

As people work on differentiation in their important systems, they often take three steps:

- Observe,
- Think, plan and rehearse, and
- Do.

1. Observe.

Observation of the system is the first important step, and we have to keep coming back to it constantly. As one observes, one is already a little "out" of the system, managing self well. One looks for emotional patterns, how the anxiety moves in the system and how one contributes to the overall level of immaturity. This data-gathering step is essential to understanding.

2. Think, plan and rehearse.

On the basis of what one sees, one is in a position to think about changes one would like to make. *These changes, of course are in the self, not in the system.*

As one sees one's contribution to the passing of emotion in patterned ways, one can plan how one would like to do things differently. For the author, it goes something like, "The next time that situation arises between him (or her) and me, I would like to. . ."

With a plan, it is necessary to rehearse it in the head. Otherwise, when the drama actually unfolds, and the cerebrum is subject to the anxiety of the system, the whole plan is forgotten.

3. Do.

Of course, if one observes and thinks all one's life, but never does anything, no differentiation of self actually takes place. That happens in the emotional field—usually in the original family where the patterns developed. One has to actually put oneself in the arena, giving oneself an opportunity to function differently and better there. It will take many trips and many tries. But the family is obliging—it has a tendency to repeat its patterns over and over. So if one doesn't perform up to expectations the first or second try, there is always another time.

As one gets more focus on self management, observing and watching one's own anxiety level,

- Relationship functioning improves.
- If leadership relationships improve, there is less anxiety in the organization.
- Relationships begin to improve organization-wide.
- This frees energy of the group to do its work.

Thinking It Over

High level leaders are working on differentiating more basic self and operating out of it more and more of the time. They work on themselves in their family emotional field as well as in the organizational setting. A leader who is working on self is an unusual, high level, attractive leader.

Real Life Research

1 Why is "differentiation" the best term to represent high level functioning?

2 What are synonyms for it?

3 What is a fusion? What are the two major types?

4 Where do we get our fusion-ability?

5 What are some synonyms for fusion?

6 What are symptoms of fusions?

7 What are characteristics of people low on the scale of differentiation?

8   What are those of people high on the scale?

9   What would be a next step up in functioning for you?

10 What would be an action plan to work on that?

11 How much of your anxiety level is relationship anxiety?

Extraordinary Relationships

We have considered the characteristics of an emotional system with its fusions, togetherness, patterns, and hierarchy. We have seen how systems press individuals into positions that are patterned. We have thought about how relationships and leadership functioning are affected by all this.

What would a relationship that was free of fusions or its patterns look like—one that was not tinged at all by togetherness symptoms? What do relationships of high level leaders look like? The following description, based on family systems theory, gives some idea.[1]

It is probably safe to assume that a perfect relationship has never existed. So while they are elusive, ideals nevertheless are useful. Experience in coaching has underscored the usefulness of clear thinking about the best that is theoretically possible. Without an idea of goals, progress is more difficult. Bowen's clear descriptions of high level functioning have greatly facilitated relationships for many. Based on those pictures, a portrait of the ideal relationship becomes possible. *It is an equal, open, and separate relationship of two high level selves.*

---

[1] See Gilbert, R., *Extraordinary Relationships,* op. cit.

A high level relationship

In the best relationships, then, there would be a greater degree of individuality and less togetherness—those innate, yet opposite forces. While relationships can fulfill the togetherness force through fusions, there is less need for fusion or togetherness at high levels. There is less tendency to fuse self with others. Thus, *individuality becomes, surprisingly, important to the success of relationships. To the degree that each partner is an individual self (emotionally separate from the other and from others in general), the relationship will be successful.*

If there were no patterns operating (only possible if no fusions are present), what would the relationship look like? Of all the characteristics of an ideal relationship, that is, one that exists at the highest level of differentiation of self, three emerge:

- Separateness of the partners emotionally (no conflict or distance)

- Equality in how they interact as selves (no over- or under-functioning)

- Openness in communications (no triangles or distance)

Separate, Equal and Open Relationship[2]

Separateness

"A more differentiated person can participate freely in the emotional sphere without the fear of becoming too fused with

---

[2] This diagram was presented at Georgetown Family Center by Dr. Roberta Holt, around 1982.

others. He or she also is free to shift to calm, logical reasoning for decisions that govern life." [3]

Partners in a well-functioning relationship lose no self into the relationship because their self boundaries are intact and their inner guidance systems well-developed. They do not take part in trading of self. They function as autonomous, individual selves in or out of the relationship. Neither relies on the other for "support," or expects the relationship to complete a part of the self perceived as lacking. Individuals at high levels of functioning need no "support." Since the self is well developed there is no need for completion of it. For this reason, it is possible for the selves to retain a separateness not seen in most relationships. That is, each has more choice about whether to respond emotionally to the other's intensities. If two individuals are emotionally separate, any anxiety one may experience does not escalate into painful interchanges or settle into emotional patterns.

In addition to being less emotionally reactive to each other, if emotionally separate, people have some ability to choose between emotions and thinking. This makes it possible for one to be calm in the face of the other's anxiety. If one person can stay calm and logical, anxiety does not escalate and circuit around the system.

Intact boundaries also mean the relationship and the system is not burdened with intense anxiety aimed at it. Each is able to manage his or her own emotions adequately by processing them. What each then contributes to the relationship is thoughtful and constructive.

If the boundaries of the self were completely intact, relationship patterns would not occur, since trading of self occurs in all the patterns.

Separateness of the selves may be an important contribution to the excitement and pleasure of new relationships. Emotional fusion or relationship patterns have not become established, so the new relationship is free of the anxiety created by patterns. It

---

[3] *Ibid*, p. 364.

sparkles like fine crystal. To the degree that emotional separateness of selves can be maintained over time, the relationship takes on radiance more like that of a diamond.

Separate, Equal and Open Relationship

Equality

The . . . self is not negotiable in the relationship system in that it is not changed by coercion or pressure, or to gain approval, or enhance one's stand with others.[4]

A high level relationship is characterized by equality. There is less trading of self. Thus, postures as overfunctioning/ underfunctioning do not occur.

A better functioning relationship is built upon equality. It does not have to be worked at, it is just there. That equality is not based on tallying up individual assets or strengths. Rather, it is a relationship stance—a posture assumed by the individuals. Each accepts the other as no more and no less talented, responsible, or free. Respect for the other, so often pointed to as essential for relationship success, is based on the equal posture. While equal partners accommodate each other and may divide up labor or tasks according to interests and ability, equality does not include emotionally patterned overfunctioning or underfunctioning.

In heading toward more equality in relationship, the principles of differentiation, thinking systems and seeing the

---

[4] Bowen, *Family Therapy, op cit* p. 473.

emotional process, point the way. To the extent that togetherness is not allowed to undo the individuality of each person, equality is not endangered. As one makes more progress toward becoming a complete and better-differentiated self, equality is less and less an issue in all relationships. There is less trading of selves into unequal postures. Keeping a constant focus on emotional process in relationships helps one know when one is beginning to take a posture that is "less than" or "more than."

Separate, Equal and Open Relationship

Openness

One of the most effective. . .mechanisms for reducing the overall level of anxiety in a family is a relatively "open" relationship system. . .An open relationship system, which is the opposite of an emotional cutoff, is one in which family members have a reasonable degree of emotional contact with one another.[5]

Openness refers to communication patterns. In a well-functioning relationship there is nothing people can't talk about. It is based on integrity—honesty—often referred to as transparency.

The complaint heard most frequently from couples seeking professional help is, "We have a communication problem!" Communication is an important and obvious part of any

---

[5] Bowen, *Family Therapy, op cit* p. 537

relationship. And, because communication is so noticeable to the people involved, it is often seen as "the problem." However, to the extent that the relationship is involved in any of the patterns, effective communication is lessened. When people work on the postures underlying their communication problems, communication improves almost automatically. Clearly, *communication is less a problem than a symptom*. The problem is the relationship posture itself.

Relationship postures are different from each other and so communication within each posture is correspondingly different. Although communication should not be mistaken for "the problem" a great deal can be learned about communication by looking at how the different patterns affect it. Conversely, by examining communication in a relationship, it's possible to identify the underlying relationship positions.

Emotional reactivity, the simplest communication

The simplest form of relationship that exists is a feeling-emotional relationship. This type of relationship based more on feelings and less on thought, is seen among animals or very young children, where thinking is less developed. There is a simple give-and-take based mostly on the emotional/feeling states of the individuals. Many adults, in their important relationships, have not progressed far beyond this simple ebb and flow of feelings and emotions, even though their thinking brain is fully developed.

In every relationship, no matter how emotionally mature, emotions are continuously signaled and received nonverbally. Facial expressions, physical postures and gestures are constantly transmitted and received. Reactivity can thus be instantly stimulated, even though it is not translated into thought or words by either party.

To move a relationship past this simple emotional level, we move to thoughtful verbal communication. And even so, non-verbal communications will always be present. It is automatic. But, thoughtful verbal communication is an important hallmark of high level relationships. In verbal expression, the emotional separation of the selfs is expressed or explained and furthered at the same time. Being more of a self means partly defining that self to the other(s) in a relationship or a relationship system. *Communication in the best relationships becomes a self-defining give and take of ideas.*

How do the various relationship postures affect verbal communications? Where a relationship pattern exists, the give and take of ideas between partners is stunted or distorted as a function of the pattern itself.

Distant communications

In the distance pattern, for example, communication is restricted. This is not to say, of course, that the partners are not interacting. There is an emotional arousal between them and interaction occurs. But the interaction is on a reactive basis and this reactivity serves only to restrict verbal communication further. Of course, it is possible for a distanced couple to appear to be open in communication, talking much but saying nothing really important to each other, carefully avoiding meaningful issues. Often such relationship partners are unaware of the distance. It is too carefully disguised by empty chatter. So, in distancing there is less and less relevant communication. There may be complete cessation of verbal communication long before actual emotional cutoff occurs. *In time, and with cutoff, there may be none.*

In optimal communication, people talk openly, with relevance and meaning, at least some of the time. What can be learned about optimal communication from the other relationship patterns?

Conflicted communications

In the conflictual relationship pattern, there is also a great deal of emotional triggering of each by the other, each projecting blame onto the other. Because of the emotional escalation that ensues, clear-headed thoughtfulness becomes extremely difficult.

Rather, each becomes embroiled in frenzied reactivity. Preoccupied with each other, thoughtful focus on self is missing. Blaming, accusative "You. . ." assertions violate boundaries. Calm, thoughtful "I think. . ." statements are missing.

Communication of ideas is dependent upon an emotionally calm brain state for reliable thought production. In conflict, there is a great deal of interaction and what might even pass for communication of ideas. But "thinking" is so emotionally based that what is really taking place is the passing back and forth of anxiety, like a ball. Words are triggered by the emotional centers of the brain. No ideas are produced that the partners would stand by over time. Therefore, a second characteristic of optimal communication is that it is *non-reactive.*

Triangled communications

Triangling, whether it is through a child, such as in a child focus, or another adult, in an affair, effectively stifles the flow of ideas between two people who are important to each other. Thinking gets generated, but it is about, to or through the third party. Since the partners make contact primarily around or through the third party, verbal communications are completely taken up with that third person.

For example, with a symptomatic child, nearly all of the parents' conversations and thinking may be taken up with worry and concern over the child. They give advice and directives to him or her continually. With a triangled adult, as in an affair, optimal communication between the primary two is impossible because the emotional reactivity engendered by the preoccupation with the third, prevents directness. Because they are not communicating with each other about self or the relationship, they are communicating mostly about someone else. So a third essential of high level communication is *directness. They need to talk to and with each other about self and the relationship.*

Over- and underfunctioning reciprocity

In an over/underfunctioning reciprocity, the communications style is one of the most easily discernable characteristics and may easily be taken as the problem. One of the partners is the "sayer" and the other the "listener." Verbal communications stay one way for the most part. The overfunctioner takes the part of chief communicator, with communications taking the forms of telling, advising, preaching, teaching, or explaining. The underfunctioner does not contribute his or her equal share in conversations.

A fourth characteristic of high level communications, therefore, is mutuality. A measure of mutuality might be that *each partner speaks and listens about an equal amount of time, over time.* Another measure would be *the degree to which people can talk to each other while remaining responsible for communicating only one's own thinking.*

The elements of high level communications

From examining the four relationship postures, then, a description of the elements of optimal communication in a significant relationship can be derived. It is *the direct, mutual, non-reactive verbal give and take of relevant thinking.*

This kind of communication is the expression of a high level relationship. It facilitates the attainment of an even better-functioning one. While it is possible to see that communications are symptomatic of the relationship patterns, they also exert an effect of their own upon the relationship, so they are well worth looking at.

Listening for each person is fifty percent of the communication process in an ideal relationship. Listening is an active process. The best listeners seem to have an ability to mentally "get in the skin" of the other, yet keep utterly calm and quiet so as to better understand what is said—one can never know what the other is thinking. They can then quickly get back into their own skin. It is impossible to have high-level communication unless both partners are skilled listeners. It is as difficult to learn to be a good listener as it is to be a clear, direct, non-reactive speaker. (On the average, it probably takes therapists at least a year of training experience to become adequate listeners.)

Insistence upon continual "dumping" of anxiety into the relationship is a destructive pattern. Traditional theory (based on a study of the individual) promotes this type of emotional expression. *However, very few relationships can withstand it.* When one can take responsibility for one's own anxiety and the processing of it, communication will be greatly enhanced.

Each is responsible for and only for self.

It's not that they don't do things for each other. They may. But doing for the other is not carried to the point of doing in the other, or becoming frozen into the rut of an over/under-functioning pattern. Neither is dependent upon the other for happiness or emotional fulfillment. *Happiness and emotional fulfillment are seen rather as responsibilities of the self, to be undertaken for the self.* Being emotionally responsible also includes managing one's emotions so as not to burden the relationship with them. *Emotional responsibility for self means not taking responsibility for the emotions of the other.* While the relationship is not without sensitivity, (awareness of the other's state) there is no need to take responsibility for the other's emotions, since each is responsible for self.

The following descriptions are most apt for important one-to-one family relationships, but they shed some light on two high-level persons relating in any situation.

The partners are "in contact."

Relationships take time. They are present with one another a sufficient amount of time. They develop an understanding of what is personally meaningful to self and to the other. Neither speaks for the other but for and only for self. Each takes responsibility for defining, interpreting, and communicating his or her own thoughts and positions to the other. Conversely, no responsibility is taken for defining or communicating the thinking or positions of the other, since the other is responsible for that.

Storytelling is an excellent way to be heard. It comes naturally to many people. Others must work to become good storytellers. The ability to spin an interesting yarn is a wonderful asset in relationships. Stories, while creative and colorful, may be overused, but they can sometimes make a lasting point without "de-selfing" anyone.

At the highest levels of relationship functioning, it is postulated that communication would have certain further characteristics, growing out of the high level of maturity of the partners. Here is a partial list:

- **Focused conversation.** Because each person is responsible for and is processing his or her own feelings, communications are free of emotionally driven tangentiality—getting off the point.

- **Creativity.** When a mutual thinking-through process operates, the thinking of each is stimulated by the thinking of the other. The partnership exerts a positive influence on the creative process of each.

- **Self-definition.** High level partners can use thinking-based communication as a self-defining process. Explaining one's thoughts to another or accurately hearing the thinking of another can be a rigorous exercise. One's stands on issues, one's ideas, and one's beliefs all come into clearer focus during such a process. Learning to only define self to another in this context will take the "you" out of most communications. Instead, communication will take place from the point of view of "I think. . ." or "It seems to me. . ."

- **Meaningfulness.** When two people experience each other as separate selves and as equals, they are free to communicate accurately what they really think to each other. This includes where they stand on issues. If they stay non-reactive, they also are freer to communicate completely, because they are relieved of emotional consequences.

In ideal relationships, the three components—emotional separateness, equality, and open communication—for most of us, remain goals rather than attainments. The effort to understand each of the three separately leads, surprisingly, to the discovery of their great degree of interdependence. The more familiar one becomes with them, the more one realizes the ideas of separateness, equality and openness can scarcely be teased apart.

For example, thinking about emotional separateness and all its implications inevitably leads to the ideas of equality and open communication. Or, as we have seen, it becomes impossible to consider openness in communication without the ideas of equality and emotional separateness coming in too. The interdependence is not merely a theoretical phenomenon, it is very practical. Working on one aspect of a relationship improves all aspects of it.

As people work toward differentiation of self, thinking systems and watching for emotional process, their relationship functioning improves steadily. With some understanding of a theory of relationships and a glimpse of the goal, it becomes possible to take a further step to see what kind of work people need to do to bring theory to life.

Leadership relationships

High level leaders are relationship masters. They relate to everyone, regardless of status, with an equal posture. Their integrity creates openness. Their impermeable boundaries do not promote anxiety flow through the system. Their relationship awareness begins at home in their families. They are a great asset to any group high enough in maturity to attract them.

Thinking It Over

A high level relationship—one that has separate boundaries, open communications, and is equal—may remain, for most of us a goal. But, even working toward it drastically changes the quality of relationships to a better level.

Real Life Research

1   How many relatively open, separate and equal relationships have you seen?

2   When you get tripped up, in which of the three areas is it?

3   Does that look like a pattern you experienced in your family growing up?

4   What can you learn by looking for high level relationships on your family diagram?

5   On the international scene, what examples of high level relationships or relating could be cited?

6   Could this way of thinking be used by peace negotiators? How?

7   Why are relationships important to leaders?

8   Describe a relationship master.

7

Extraordinary Leadership

What is a high level leader? How do we know when we see one? And how do we know when we're making strides toward becoming that Extraordinary Leader we would all like to become?

High level leaders are high on the scale of differentiation of self. That being the case, let's think about the ideas contained in that concept as they apply to those in a leadership position.

First, a look at low level leadership will clarify what we're trying to avoid (and what we see in the news all too often).

Low level leadership

Low level leaders are low on the scale of differentiation of self. That means they are anxious, intense people, because low levels on the scale carry with them a higher ambient level of anxiety. *They are fused into their important relationships, an uncomfortable state that produces even more anxiety*, depending on how the relationships are going. The relationship anxiety and fusions of this leader will wreak havoc in the system. The relationship postures and patterns are characteristic of this leader. We'll consider each of them in turn.

The overfunctioning leader

Overfunctioning leaders give a lot of orders, telling people how and what to think. They are the tyrants. They demand that people do what they say, supporting the leader in every respect, or else. People must unquestioningly think as they think. Dialogue is out of the question at the lowest levels. Directives and ideas are one-way: "Do it because I say so" The reciprocity involved in relating in this way means that they pay back, with favors and positions, friends who have helped them regardless of their ability to do the job. This is known in the natural world and written about as altruism.[1] In like manner, revenge is common, as when Saddam Hussein, Stalin, Lenin and many others promptly shot all their opposition when they took over.

The overfunctioner:

- Bullies with loud and constant talk, promoting groupthink in this way,
- Knows all the answers,
- Doesn't delegate enough and overworks,
- Is a poor listener,
- Has to have all the ideas,
- Is easily threatened.

The overfunctioning leader takes responsibility for the group. Bowen learned about this the hard way in his research years at the National Institutes of Health: *"In the early stages of family research, a good percentage of my time went into thinking about problems in the staff and in the families, and offering solutions. This worked very well but everyone was dependent on me for suggesting solutions and the staff was not developing in the direction of assuming responsibility for their own solutions. It was then that I discovered I was in fact being irresponsible in my own functioning in other areas. My effort went into clarification*

---

[1] Trivers, R., *Natural Selection and Social Theory: Selected Papers of Robert Trivers,* Chapter 1 p. 3, "Reciprocal Altruism," Oxford University Press, London, 2002.

of my responsibility as head of the research, and functioning responsibly there, without assuming responsibility for others. Very quickly I learned that if there was an emotional issue in the organization, I was playing a part in it, and if I could modify the part I was playing, the others would do the same. This principle has been used through the years in my own family, in my clinical work, and in my administrative functioning. Any time one key member of an organization can be responsibly responsible for self, the problem in the organization will resolve." [2]

If, rather than complaining about their organizations' functioning, leaders would look through the systems lens at themselves, seeing how they are playing their part in the problem, and changing that, they would, over time, see a very different organization.

But leaders can also take the opposite posture, one of underfunctioning.

Underfunctioning

Leaders, as well as anyone else, can automatically by their anxiety and immaturity, underfunction in relationships, taking weak postures that feel and act out of "I can't," "I don't know," or "I'm not adequate." They may have no idea of how to assist a group to organize itself. Thus, group emotional process spins out of control. Or they themselves may be disorganized, forgetting meetings or showing up late. They may not prepare for presentations or ramble when in front of the group. They may put off making decisions far too long, or not make them at all. They may ask for consultations or advice they would not need if they would take the time to think through issues, using the lens of systems theory. They may become symptomatic, making it even more difficult to function in their roles.

---

[2] Bowen, M., *Family Therapy,* op. cit., p. 463.

Conflict

If a leader's anxiety takes the form of conflicted relationships, there will be a never-ending stream of issues to feed it. There is always something to oppose. The initiation of conflict can come from the leader or from a member of the group. It takes forms such as;

- Reflexive opposition or disagreeing,

- Constant competing or "one-upmanship,"

- Criticizing: finding fault with all ideas except one's own regardless of their actual merit,

- Assigning blame, and

- Nit-picking—in short,

- Opposing.

If a leader is prone to conflictual posture, he or she will be ineffectual, always increasing the emotional intensity of the group. On the other hand, if a member succeeds in triggering the leader to conflict, the outcome is the same. With thinking minimized, there will be no forward movement.

Distance

Though distance is present in all the patterns, it can also stand as a posture in its own right.

Even when there are legitimate reasons for the distance, such as family illness, a group finds it difficult to cope with an absent leader, whether physically or emotionally. Anxiety rises and then any number of the relationship postures and patterns become apparent. Distance can be more subtle than geographic distance, however. It can take the form of:

- Not answering phone or e-mail messages,

- "Being somewhere else" during a meeting—being preoccupied,

- Not listening carefully,
- Changing the subject if things become a little sensitive,
- Not taking part in conversations—or listening too much, shutting down, and taking a passive role,
- Neglecting to maintain important relationships, e.g., with one's own leadership or with community peers and leaders, and/or
- Being called out unavoidably and finding no way to stay connected during the absence.

With a distant leader, the group is at loose ends, getting nothing done, or else going off in several ineffective directions. Both group and leader become more and more anxious the longer the distant posture continues.

Interestingly, one research study actually found that pastors on sabbatical did better and were more energized for their work upon their return, if they found ways to be connected during their absences, such as by e-mail or phone, with their congregations, from time to time. It was the ones who totally "got away from it all" with no communication, that had no energy upon their return.[3]

Triangling

A leader may take anxiety from meetings and relationships, inappropriately, into other relationships. This can take the form of:

- Talking about people when they are not there,
- Worrying about someone's responsibilities that are not one's own instead of observing, showing confidence or discussing issues as equals,
- Gossip and rumors,

---

[3] Hay, T "A Difference in Experience on Sabbatical" available on website www.hsystems.org

- Too intense friendships or other relationships with congregation members,

- Telling one's spouse confidential information.

Groups resent the lack of directness when a leader triangles. They in turn will do the same and things go quickly out of control as the triangles build and interlock.

In short, low level leaders operate out of their lower level on the scale. Sometimes overfunctioners can be quite effective—for awhile. But the group will rebel in time, or they will become very tired of someone "over" them, being "irresponsibly responsible." Or they may just glide into a chronic underfunction where there is no energy and nothing ever gets done. The leaders will want to move on, the group will overthrow them, or they may become victim to burnout or sudden illness.

Underfunctioners and distancers can delegate all their responsibility to others—for awhile. But eventually everyone in this arrangement wears thin. The organization wants a leader who is there, thinking and interacting with them. Conflictual leaders may have the shortest tenure of all. Intense explosions or constant conflict in the group tends to wear out a group rather rapidly.

The emotions/intellect fusion

The other fusion found at the lower end of the scale of differentiation, that of intellect and emotions, means that leaders with lower levels of differentiation do not think too clearly. Their thinking, fired by emotion, is partial, scattered, vindictive, under active, tangential, oppositional, preoccupied, unfocused, over-critical, or unreliable.

This emotional firing of the intellect results in poor decision-making. So this leader, and his or her organization, will reap an undue number of problems as a result. Bad decisions have a way of multiplying themselves, in a downward spiral that feeds on itself.

Another untoward result of the intellect/emotion fusion can be the tendency to take action too soon—impulsivity. In some people their anxiety cries out for them to take action though the issues are unresolved and the action not completely thought through. These actions can lead to predicaments of immense proportions that often have long term consequences.

High level leaders

Of course, leaders, like all people, exist at all levels on the scale of differentiation. Thus, more often than the extremes described, we see gradations and nuances of them. But the extremes are useful for instruction. They illustrate where we want to go and where we don't. Most of us will fall somewhere in-between those descriptions, some higher and some lower.

The low level traps teach a great deal, but what is leadership of a different level—what is high level leadership? What does it look like? By knowing something about that, we are in a better position to shoot for it.

Less anxiety

Since they carry around less anxiety on a daily basis, high level leaders are able to relate more "out" of the postures and patterns. And since they have more intact self boundaries, they take on less anxiety from others. Their relationships will display less **overfunctioning**, they:

- Treat individuals as equals,
- Talk no more or less than they listen,
- Don't insist that their ideas have to be adopted, but
- Allow enough time for the thinking-through process of the group, knowing a good decision is a process,
- Listen carefully, and
- Encourage good thinking and creative ideas.

They function as expected by not **underfunctioning**—they:

- Are on time for meetings and appointments,
- Prepare for meetings, talks, presentations, thoroughly,
- Attend to their health, physical, mental/emotional and social,
- Hold up their end of the conversations in meetings and other dialogue,
- Say what they think,
- Don't allow the group to highjack the leader's responsibilities.

High functioning leaders stay out of **conflict** as a pattern. Though they may disagree—they:

- Know that "a soft answer turneth away wrath,"
- Know when to take a break to let the emotional intensity cool down,
- Keep the big picture through humor, calming exercises such as slow deep breathing, and prayer,[4]
- Observe themselves and the group process for intensity, thinking about what is triggering them,
- Know the value of cooperation but don't get into groupthink,
- Know that there are always other ways to see an issue than conflictually.

Distancing is not in the repertoire of the high functioning leader. He or she:

- Stays active and involved, especially intellectually,
- Finds ways to stay connected if he or she has to be away,

---

[4] Harrison, V "A Study of Prayer and Human Reactivity" can be ordered from www.hsystems.org .

- Makes adequate provision for tasks being carried out if gone,
- Keeps thinking and focused, listening carefully during meetings and conversations,
- Answers messages,
- Gets back with answers if agrees to—is a resource to the group,
- Consults appropriate people,

Triangles, always present, are managed. The high level leader:

- Talks to both angles of a triangle, showing confidence in their relating abilities,
- Keeps confidences,
- Makes calming contact with trianglers—not necessarily about "the issue" or "the rumor,"
- Keeps relationships one-to-one,
- "Thinks systems" to figure out what is going on,
- Thinks theory to determine the best course of action if the triangles start to interlock,

Relationship masters

High level leaders are "relationship masters." That is, they keep their boundaries separate from others, knowing their guiding principles as well as limitations. They are able to define these to the group, as and when they can be heard. They relate to others as equals. They are not carried away by their positions, using them to wield power over others. And they do not expect others to do their job for them. They are open and direct in interactions, saying what needs to be said. If they stop and think about it, theory tells them what that is.

Clear thinkers

Because they have less emotion/thinking fusion, they are clearer thinkers. When the group threatens to be awash in emotion, with very little reliable, logical, fact based thinking going on, the high level leader is a great resource. He or she can define a logical way of thinking about a matter or ask a question based on facts, putting the group back on a more solid thoughtful process—one that is likely to get to some resolution.

Ability to "stay out" emotionally

While a high level leader can empathize long enough to see how the other must be feeling, he or she can also "get out" of the other's emotional states fast, into his or her own head and calmer emotional state. He or she does not allow the emotional state of the other or of the group to determine his or her own state. This ability, *to stay calm when others are not—to choose one's mood—is the mark of a person functioning at a high level on the scale.* It is also a great resource to the organization or congregation high enough on the scale to attract such a person as leader. Like anxiety, calm is infectious too (though it is a slower process). When even one person in a group, especially the leader, can determine his or her own emotional state—stay "apart" emotionally from the group—the whole group steps up and does better, both at the time, and over time.

High level leaders know, or learn, how to relax. Muscular relaxation is incompatible with anxiety.

How family systems theory is about leadership

The subject of leadership arises at least two ways in Bowen family systems theory. The first is in its view of parents as the leaders of the nuclear family. The second place leadership comes into view is as a natural outcome of building more basic self through differentiation efforts.

First, parents as leaders of the family

Because organizations and emotional systems are in many ways, homologous with the nuclear family, and parents are the natural leaders of the family, parents become an instructive paradigm for leadership. This does not mean that a high level leader in an organization treats people in the organization as if they were children. The goal of a high functioning parent is to produce an adult who interacts with others, one day including Mom or Dad, as an equal. A high functioning parent relates to children more and more as equals, the older they become.

So a high functioning leader, dealing with adults, will interact with members of the organization as equals. Their place on the organizational chart does not influence the way the leader interacts with them.

This leader will interact with staff in the same way. Although, as we have seen, there is probably never equality in any organization, the leader who makes the effort to interact equally with all in it in a level manner finds a great deal of energy and creativity coming from groups that others, who bully or tower over, or under, in their relationships, do not.

Leadership relationships need time

Parents who do not work out their relationship problems between themselves create anxiety that will spill out to the rest of the family, creating over focus, which often leads to symptoms.

In the same way, *leaders who do not take the time to talk over and work out real or perceived issues as they arise, getting to resolution, create anxiety that will spill through the triangles to the rest of the organization.* It can result in firings, leavings, fights, or people who don't do their jobs well.

High level parents sometimes have to say "no"

At times, immature sectors of the group threaten to tyrannize it. When that happens, like well-functioning parents, leadership can process issues, join together and set limits for what the group

103

will and will not tolerate, what group guidelines must be followed, or what is acceptable behavior.

Immature or anxious adults, like children, do not like this process, just *as the best parents are not liked all the time*. It is not the goal of parents to always be liked, unless they are extremely immature themselves. If the leadership stays on course, the reaction to the limit-setting will be short lived. People gradually step up to higher functioning under the guidance of leaders who are willing to do their job in this respect, not in a bullying or tyrannical sort of way, but with facts and the more mature leadership of the group working together with them.

This is not an unequal posture as much as it is the maturity of the group (the higher level leaders) taking a stand—a position that defines limits.

The I position

When a family goes into a "regression" (high anxiety levels and poor functioning), it can pull out by *one parent taking a stand for higher and better functioning*. The "I statement" in such a case is something like: "This group can do better and this is what can be expected of me in the future." When one can pull up and out of the regression the rest of the group follows.

The same is true of an organization. If the leader can give a clear message, take a stand, "These are my (or the group's, according to their principles) limits and boundaries and this is what can be expected if this behavior continues," others will follow and the regression will terminate. The I position is not a focus on others. It is a statement of the organization's boundaries, according to its principles.

Second, stepping up in one's family of origin

The second paradigm for leadership in Bowen theory is differentiation itself. With coaching, and over time, people who take family systems theory seriously work on gaining more self and improving their relationships in their families of origin. It is the most important effort in Bowen theory. Bowen discovered that people who did this work gained benefits that could be obtained in no other way. People working on themselves in their families of origin find that they become leaders there. They do not become leaders by setting out to lead anyone but themselves. Rather, as they get better relationships with those in their families, they become "attractive." People seek them out for advice and counseling, for their thinking or for important family roles that can best carried out by them.

The increase in level of basic self, gained in working on oneself in one's family of origin, cannot help but improve functioning in all areas, including that of leadership. It also becomes a paradigm for leadership functioning.

Growing more basic self automatically results in a higher level leader.

High level leadership is attractive

Leaders, like people working to become more of a self in their families, can do the same sort of work in their organizations. This is not a substitute for doing the family work, but the two efforts go hand in hand. *As one steps up in functioning in one's family, one does so in one's organization.* One can also work for better relationships in one's organization, and do better in one's family as a result. As that occurs, people notice. They are attracted.

Why are high level people attractive to others? For one thing, their low level of anxiety gives them a comfort level that others want to be around to absorb. (Emotional states are "catching.") Anxiety is difficult to be around. When people find a calm person, they want to be near them—the emotional state they radiate is one that others would like.

For another, it is intriguing to find someone who knows what they think and is guided by principle. If one believes in his or her guiding principles enough to be calm for them, others sense that this is a high level person who has done some serious thinking about important issues. They want to know more of what and how this unusual person thinks. They want his or her counsel.

They make requests for important functions that they know are best done by this high level leader.

Extraordinary Leaders are open communicators

High level leaders are original, independent thinkers who can clearly define their thinking to the group when appropriate. These "definitions of self" are dependent on a connectedness with many others in the congregation or smaller groups. They are based on the guiding principles of self and those of the group.

As we have seen, knowledge of the relationship patterns can often prevent communications difficulties. Theory works also to show leaders how to communicate one-on-one within the organization. They:

- Are open, finding most things can be talked over with benefit to all if one does not betray confidences, try to get in control, get "done in," fight, or distance,
- Listen carefully and then represent themselves accurately and calmly,
- Choose their words well, to accurately reflect thinking
- Try to keep the big picture.

Systems thinking, invaluable to the leader

Systems thinking has transformed the functioning of so many people, including leaders, that it is difficult to stay calm about it.

However, like any other worthwhile effort, it takes time and effort to become facile at thinking systems. Three years in a didactic program that includes coaching is a minimum for a serious effort. More serious students stay with programs longer. Even at that, *most people find that if they do not keep contact with others who are well trained in systems thinking, frequently and regularly, they can quickly lose their gains.* Most programs design a way for serious long term systems thinkers, to stay in touch with the ideas.

Coaching, by someone who has been thinking systems longer, will be an integral part of any effort to grow more self. Over time, the coaching does not, for most, need to be frequent. It takes time on the calendar to change.

Why does it take so much time and effort to be a systems thinker? Probably for several reasons. Most of us automatically think, "cause and effect." We look for someone to blame. These are ingrained neural pathways. Seeing the big picture that family systems theory opens up is foreign to many of us. The culture we live in promotes the old thoughts patterns as well.

People change but slowly. Probably major change in the structure and function of the brain is involved. That will simply take time. *In order to accomplish the major change of neuronal pathways needed for systems thinking, it takes study, time, and effort in one's own systems.* It is, however, an extremely worthwhile effort.

The most important effort

High level leaders see working on self in their family relationship systems, both in their original and in their nuclear families, as the most important work they do. As they keep that perspective, they talk of being more grounded, calmer and less apt to be triggered in the organization.

In addition, the family effort teaches them how to conduct themselves in the organization. With the ongoing family work in place, however, leadership in the organization takes on a new ease, in time. All the lessons learned and changes made in the family are carried on in their organizations.

Differentiation in an organization?

Although the family work is paramount, many see themselves doing better in their organizations by being guided by family systems ideas as they step up in functioning there. The same differentiation efforts that one makes in the family can be replicated in organizations, too.

As leaders work on being more of a self and on better relationships with those in their organizations as well as with those over them in their particular hierarchies, they see a new, better, easier, more comfortable leadership style emerging within themselves. They don't get as tired. They are more sure. They see a direction more of the time.

Guidance by principle

Though relationships are important to high level leaders, their actions and decisions are not guided by them. They have within, a guidance system, made up of well thought through principles that serve them well. They may not talk about these principles much, but others do find them very interesting when they bring them out, at the right time and place. They do not hit people over the head with them, but they are no secret, either. When the occasion calls for it, high level leaders find a way to describe the thinking that guides them.

It is refreshing to find a leader today that is guided by principle, partly because it is so rare. It is part of what sets apart the high from the low level leaders, who lead by relationships or emotions.

Thinking It Over

High level leaders are high on the scale of differentiation. They lead by principle, but are relationship masters and great communicators. They know how to calm their emotions in order to think more clearly. They are attractive and people want to know more of what they think and how they operate.

Real Life Research

1. Have you ever known a high level leader?

2. Give some current or historical examples of leaders who lead or led by relationships or emotions.

3. How do high functioning parents lead their families? Have you known some?

4. What is the most important work an aspiring high level leader can do?

5. Why do you think systems thinking is so hard to learn?

6. How does a leader assist a system toward more openness?

7. What are some of your guiding principles?

8. What is a relationship master?

9. Can you name some high level leaders from history?

10. What work in your family, in your organization do you see to do on self as a next step toward high level leadership?

8

Formal Communications

Of all the difficulties that leaders have in communicating their ideas publicly, the most frequent and important culprit is that of their own anxious posture.[1] Because anxiety in the speaker is transmitted to the entire audience, it interferes with both hearing and understanding. If we, as teachers, speakers or writers, contribute in some way to the difficulty people have in hearing us, that is a part we have the power to change.

When writing or speaking, we may get all the words down in a way that is technically what we wanted to say, yet unnecessarily difficult to hear or comprehend. In that case the receiver takes away from our message, not what we meant to convey, but rather, confusion, lack of understanding, upset, or boredom. The message is not understood though the actual words may have been clear and accurate. The next account, upon repetition, by the listener of what was said may be far from what was actually said or intended by the speaker/writer. In this way, some strange ideas can be put into circulation.

---

[1] This chapter is adapted from an article published in *Family System Forum*, a publication of the Center for the Study of Natural Systems and the Family, Houston, Austin, and El Paso, Texas, requested and edited by Rev. Katie Long.

For example, the author once asked three people at a conference what a certain speaker had said, explaining she had not understood his message. (The speaker was an especially boring one.) Each of the three gave a completely different report of what the talk was about.

How does this happen? I think theory can explain it. As has often been pointed out, speaking in public is a common fear. And because writing also involves an audience, perhaps it is not far behind. Writing can be even more daunting since written words carry with them permanence, and often an even larger audience. This anxiety, so much a part of speaking and writing, can interfere with clear communications in two ways. First, *anxiety can trigger relationship patterns in speakers and writers.* Second, *anxiety interferes with thinking.*

Clergy people get plenty of practice in speaking (and writing too) so they may not actually be triggered into anxiety by formal communications. However, they may be carrying around anxiety from the congregational relationships or their own family that interferes with the quality of the spoken or written message. Let us examine different ways that anxiety can work against getting out our messages clearly.

Anxious Patterns

When anxious, people tend to revert to automatic patterns— whether they know systems theory or not. Of course, there are attempts to relieve the anxiety. While they may relieve the speaker's anxiety, *they can affect the audience's ability to hear and understand.* These patterned ways of reacting in anxious relationships are: distance, conflict, over- and underfunctioning, and triangling.

What do these patterns have to do with speaking or writing? Only that, at their best, speaking and writing are more than educating or informing. They are, in addition, when excellent, *a relationship—a connection—with each person in the audience or with the reader.* Further, if the speaker or writer does not relate to his or her audience in the best way possible, the message very likely will not be heard at all. So *the best speaker or writer is good at relationships*. Most of us, though, even if we are pretty good at relationships in everyday life, find that the anxiety associated with public communications interferes with representing self as well as we might like. So we find ourselves getting into the automatic patterns without ever knowing it.

Distance

The commonest pattern the author notices in self and others in speaking is that of distance. It can be evoked by getting into the fused posture. This happens most often by too much talk in personal pronouns where "you and I" or "you" are referred to frequently. The audience automatically distances from the frank attempt at an over close relationship that is not warranted.

Another common way to distance from an audience is to *read one's talk, never looking up* (from the paper or the laptop) at the audience. In this way listeners are shut out so one doesn't have to deal with them. (When we do look up, we wonder why so many in the audience bury themselves in note-taking.)

Another too-often heard device that is a distancing maneuver, is the *sing-song*. In that one, the voice rises and falls at predictable times in each sentence rather than when the meaning of the thought would naturally indicate emphasis. It has the non-verbal, unintended effect of making the talk seem meaningless. When the message is robbed of meaning, the sing-song acts as a lullaby, and the audience goes to sleep. Again, with distance established, the speaker doesn't have the anxiety of people watching.

Still another lullaby for an audience is that of the *monotone*, where the voice never rises or falls, emphasizing nothing at all, giving the anxious impression, "What I'm saying is not as important as getting this over with." The non-verbal, automatic, emotional message given to the audience is that since the speaker does not think the message important, it isn't. Since *speakers are emotionally influential,* the audience will tend to agree and again, obligingly go off to la la land. The speaker is relieved of the responsibility of relating to them.

Because there is distance in all these devices, any of them will work to put up a wall between the speaker/writer and his or her audience. But the message is neglected, wasting the speaker's as well as many other people's time.

The same thing can occur by speaking in too soft a volume, too fast, or dropping volume at the end of sentences, so the audience does not hear a few of the words.

Conflict

Speakers are sometimes intense, angry, conflicted or competitive under pressure. They, of course, will trigger conflict in the audience.

More often, speakers are triggered into conflict. This happens commonly when a speaker or writer is defining a new or unfamiliar thought or guiding principle. He or she may have thought it through carefully, taking a stand. But if what is being said does not jibe with what the audience has always been led to, or wants to, believe, conflict can erupt during the discussion period. Some people react intensely to anything new or different. Listeners can find hearing someone defining self difficult for many reasons. The message may be different from what they have previously thought and always been taught, or what our culture is steeped in. Defining oneself may then be experienced by the listeners as counterintuitive. When reactivity to difference or newness displays itself, the speaker can take on the anxiety of the participant, becoming a ready partner in the combat. He or she may argue with the audience or react defensively or competitively. This, of course, escalates emotional process in the room, defeating any possibility of thoughtful consideration.

We all know speakers whose discussion periods are more a signal for an argument than thoughtful discourse. Others handle the discussion period with ease, relating well to even the hostile questions.

Overfunctioning

Overfunctioning speakers can adopt a know-it-all attitude, telling people what to do instead of defining self. They may use the occasion to promote self, grandstanding.

The know-it-all is arrogant; demanding by his or her attitude that the audience accept what is being said, "Because I said so." He or she gives little supporting documentation or reasoning that would assist the listener in understanding the thinking.

Preaching can be done without being "preachy," telling others what and how to think. One hears speakers who, as systems thinkers, should know better, telling others what to do or think. A tell-tale of the position is the frequent use of the word "you" as in "you should" rather than "I think."

Still other over-functioning speakers promote themselves, rather than ideas, facts, or logic or, running on about their fascinating history, exploits, or interventions. They are also prone to name dropping, showing what important friends or clients they have and thus, by association, how important they themselves are. It is a "big me, little you" position.[2] It implies, "What I have to say should be accepted without question because I am an authority." Some people, just by being in front, seem to gain self or "cheap energy."[3] There is no equality there.

Underfunctioning

The underfunctioning speaker will use overt distancing mechanisms already referred to, be late, forget to show up entirely, use bad grammar, or inappropriate vernacular. He or she may do little or no preparation for the presentation, not time the presentation, so as to not have enough material, or go over the time allotted, not getting to complete the content. He or she may speak too softly, or drop the voice at the end of sentences. The audience is left to guess at what was said.

---

[2] A favorite expression of Andrea Maloney Schara.
[3] *Ibid.*

Triangling

Triangling in public can be embarrassing or trying, as for example, when people tell stories about others without their permission. Sometimes people talk about other more interesting places or audiences where they have been or insist on quoting Bowen or other authorities every other sentence. Some presentations are almost entirely quotes from others' work with very little of the author's thinking anywhere to be found. The audience becomes annoyed. They came to hear a self speak for self.

Writing

Does writing translate into relationship terms also? It does seem that all of these speaking difficulties can be translated into written relationship problems also.

For example, how about authors that put the audience to sleep? Or one that spells out detail to a degree that diminishes the reader? Or what about the author one wants to fight back, or the one who quotes everyone and never gives any thinking of his or her own, like a bad term paper? Then of course, there are the authors who use their writing primarily as an occasion to show how clever or helpful they are in their consultations. Their writing is more about themselves, building their practices, business or egos, than about the purported subject. Their emotional process speaks so loudly we cannot hear what they are saying.

It is clear that either writing or speaking are done in the context of a relationship—that with the reader or the listener. And, although that is the case, it seems that many presenters and authors are not thinking about the occasion as a real and special relationship with specific living and thinking people. But, just as is the case in other life relationships, if one is anxious, the well-known relationship postures will become apparent. If one is operating out of one of those postures, it soon becomes evident in the communication; that, after all, cannot help but carry the emotional tone and posture of the communicator. When intense and inappropriate, people tune out the communicator along with his or her message, which becomes more distant, and perhaps then, distorted, because *distance is in all the postures.*

Anxiety interferes with thinking

Exchanging information is the purpose of communication. It is very much a thinking process. Communicating about something important (what one is saying is important or one wouldn't be going to the trouble) demands the best thinking abilities of both presenter and listener/reader.

Anxiety, however, interferes with reliable, logical thinking. The relationship postures increase anxiety, rather than resolving it, adding to the difficulty of both presenting and hearing ideas. So by adding to the anxiety, we defeat the possibility of being heard accurately. If the presenter or the author is anxious, that anxiety will be transmitted. The words become harder to grasp, less accessible and more easily misunderstood.

Thinking theory about communicating

Thinking theory assists one with these dilemmas. *If we know theory, we can use it, if we don't, we can't.* It shows the way out of most communications snafus, which are really relationship difficulties.

If a speaker maintains an *equal* posture with the listener/reader, he or she will not be in an overfunctioning mode that puts the other in a more anxious, underfunctioning position where it is more difficult to think and hear. The speaker will leave ample time for discussion.

If one maintains *boundaries* one won't go off the subject (misusing others' time or interest) or over the time allotment (invading time allotted to others). Better self boundaries also make for better focus during the talk or writing. They also mean the anxiety of the other won't automatically be absorbed.

Relationship *openness* makes it possible to explore the subject in an honest, interesting way that assumes that I want to

117

do the same good job the listener wants me to do. All this comes through in either the formally written or spoken word.

What do I do?

If anxiety is such a big part of the problem in poor communications, one can take responsibility for it, consciously working to calm down ahead of time. After all, the speaker/writer is in an emotionally influential place for a number of people.

Why not use some of those relaxation techniques many of us work so hard to learn before presenting or sitting down to the keyboard to write? *How many poor presentations would be avoided if the speaker just took ten deep, slow breaths, relaxing and releasing all anxiety, before taking the podium?*

Rehearsing oral presentations out loud ahead of time helps to stay in one's own time boundaries. Taping and listening to one's presentation can reveal distancing or other postures. A talk sounds different out loud from the way it reads.

Asking several colleagues who are knowledgeable about theory to read written work and give feedback can reveal weaknesses or misrepresentations. A reading by someone who doesn't know much about the subject can be even more useful. A professional editor can be a great investment in one's writing proficiency, teaching about clarity, usage, economy of words and telling the story in an interesting way.

Simply reading and rereading one's own writing, looking for the relationship postures is invaluable. Even though the material may have been rewritten many times, a final, critical rereading will usually show up the postures if they exist. Communicating will be from pseudo instead of basic self. In reading the galley proofs for *Extraordinary Relationships,* the author found some of the writing to be pretty good. Some of it, though, was absolutely soporific. One could not go to press with this state of affairs. Shortly, it became apparent that the sleep-inducing passages were merely what had been taught by others but not put into practice in life. They were not yet a part of basic self. All those parts had to be removed or reworked. "What does one really believe? What is a part of self and what is not?" Though anything done in the tremendously complicated English language is rarely if ever perfect, this often overlooked measure, a final rereading, or two or three, go far towards making an important message clearer and more accurately received.

In short, communicating to audiences and readers is one more opportunity to put one's most important ideas into practice and words—to be a better version of self in a relationship.

Thinking it Over

The best communications are made from an equal, open and separate posture. When emotional patterns based in anxiety and immaturity don't get in the way, one is more likely to think clearly and be heard accurately.

Real Life Research

1. How does anxiety interfere with speaking?

2. What are some of the ways this works out?

3. How do relationship principles assist in better communications?

4. What patterns are you aware of in your own speaking or writing?

5. How does reading and re-reading multiple times improve one's communications efforts?

PART III

THE SELF IN THE SYSTEM

—Contemporary Leadership

"In a small or large social system, the move toward individuality is initiated by a single, strong leader with the courage of his convictions who can assemble a team, and who has clearly defined principles on which he can base his decisions when the emotional opposition becomes intense"

Source for quotes on preceding page: Murray Bowen, *Family Therapy and Clinical Practice*, Aronson, 1978, pp. 279.

Clergy Leadership in Today's Systems

We have considered the system. We have looked at the self. Now, let us put it all together—the self in the system. Today's world can pose special challenges. We will not take up many specific issues, since "the issue is rarely the issue." But some broad categories, seen through the lens of family systems theory, may be useful as examples.

But first, let us flesh out further the idea of high level leaders. What are some of their characteristics? Extraordinary Leaders in systems are:

- Competent

- Relationship masters

- Problem-solvers

- Facilitators and promoters of guiding principles

- Vision, mission and purpose facilitators and promoters

- Networkers with the wider system, neighborhood and world

Let us look at each of these in turn.

Competent

High level leaders have a basic education that prepares them for their profession. If they are high on the scale, they probably did well in school. This is not to say that everyone who does well in school is high on the scale of differentiation, however. And not all high achievers in life are high on the scale, either. A look at other areas of the lives of some of them often shows that in relationships in their families they may be lacking.

They make a point of practicing their professions according to their guiding principles. Their principles are brought into decision making, relationships with personnel, and planning for the future, though not in an overt, frontal style.

And they stay abreast of their field. Although, because of their own guiding principles, they may not be where the field is, they stay aware and conversant with the thinking and trends in their area. Many of us need to constantly define where we stand vis à vis our professions. For example, when the major drug companies got into the area of continuing education for doctors, many saw this as a wonderful thing. The author was consistently and sometimes vocally, opposed to it. Studies are now beginning to expose how the companies skew research studies to their own advantage. It has been and is quite obvious that they do this in the "continuing education" of the medical profession. They are "teaching" doctors, not the big picture, based on all the facts, but only what they want them to think (and prescribe).

In the same way, theological, business, and educational trends come and go. These emphases (one wonders who decides what the next one will be) can be examined, held up against guiding principles, facts and knowledge and one can determine, over time, whether trends are more than just a passing fancy.

If one doesn't stay current with what is happening in one's field, one will miss out on some interesting conversations and perhaps, lose the chance to be a self in either affirming them, or in taking a stand. In other words, one can get "cut off" from one's field. Bowen theory doesn't tell us what to believe. It does endorse the value of knowing what our beliefs are and continually working on clarifying them.

Writing, a discipline for most of us in school, is sadly lacking for many later on. But it affords one of the best ways to clarify thinking, sharpening competence in the process.

There are many avenues to continue one's education. Everyone's menu differs but finding a way to attain and increase competence over the years will, for Extraordinary Leaders, include family systems training and continued seminars and conferences, since they will help keep the head on track and:

- Clear to do better work,

- Out of relationship turmoil,

- Grounded emotionally, and

- Thinking systems.

Relationship masters

Extraordinary Leaders have mastered some important relationship principles. And they keep them in mind as they interact with others. Probably not everyone needs to learn about high level relating in class. A very few, high on the scale, automatically relate to others out of an ample basic self.

Most of us, however, came out of our families with many blind spots and patterned ways of reacting. We need all the training we can get on the subject of human interactions. Especially do those of us who are serving in positions of leadership within organizations, need the guidance of principles and practice in becoming, to ourselves, and to the organization, more of who and what we want to be. Family systems theory is a welcome compass and guidebook for relationships.

High level leaders, understanding the patterned ways of relationship functioning—conflict, distance, over- and under-functioning, and triangling—are always watching for them. They observe them in others. And they can correct their own contribution to the patterns in their own relationships as they arise. They aim for relating to everyone as an eyeball-to-eyeball *equal.* Having been given a position of leadership, they do not lord it over others, becoming their boss. On the other hand, they do not become afraid of their position, not knowing what to do, going into an underfunctioning posture. When the leader interacts as an equal with others, he or she has little relationship distress to deal with. As an equal with everyone, the interactions play it out.

Their integrity gives them a transparency that people recognize, respect, relate to and emulate. They are *open* in their attitude and in their communication. They are easy to talk to, because they listen. They say what they think in a way that can be heard and when the time is right.

They have boundaries that *separate* themselves from others. This means they can define where they stand when necessary and in a calm, gentle way. It means they can define what they will and will not do without defiance. Their guiding principles are a calming influence to them and they refer to them often. They don't take on others' anxiety, nor do they spread theirs around the system. They don't become victims of "groupthink" when the group anxiety might dictate it.

Problem solvers

Extraordinary leaders' principles point the way out of dilemmas when they arise. Though they do not force them on the rest of the group, they can usually see some rather creative solutions for difficult situations. (Problem-solving is another way of saying creativity.) Some keys to this ability are:

- They manage self,
- They connect with others during the process—they are present and accounted for,
- They're curious, asking thoughtful questions,
- They observe, and
- They define their thinking to the group.

Let's consider each of these as they relate to problem-solving.

1. Self management

Above all, Extraordinary Leaders continually manage themselves. Partly this is necessary because of the immaturity we each bring to our positions. The thoughtful and differentiated part of us has a big job in managing the more emotional and undifferentiated part which has a tendency to veer out of control regularly. This is especially the case when a group is trying to solve problems.

Partly, it is necessary to manage self because group functioning, as triangled and intense as it can become, will tend to trigger the immaturity and anxiety of the leader on a regular basis. Members of the group may focus their anxiety on the leader directly or through the triangles, becoming critical, blaming or accusatory.

It is difficult to maintain a calm emotional state while connected to intensity in others. If the leader can do just that, however, not taking on the anxiety of the group, and thus, not becoming de-selfed, continuing to think and interact in conversation, the group will, in time, with its leader, go on to a better level of functioning. It will find problem-solving easier.

2. They connect with others.

In a problem-solving process, a group can become quite intense. The issue may be raising money, building, growing, the Old Guards' entitlement vs. the Newbies' great ideas—it doesn't matter—problems tend to raise the anxiety. An Extraordinary Leader, not taking on the anxiety but connecting rationally and logically with everyone concerned will be a great asset as the effort unfolds. He or she is like a breath of fresh air to the whole organization.

Some of the most anxious of the group may need a bit of extra time with the leader, just to absorb some of his or her calm and confident attitude. No one wants to connect with others who are anxious and spewing it around the group in meetings.

127

However, it is part of the job description of the leader. Certain people will simply need more time with him or her from time to time. When they meet, they may not even talk about the current problem. They may just have lunch and joke, or talk of their kids' feats. It is, most of the time, *simply connecting* that is useful to defusing the anxiety. If "the issue" of the day does come up, the leaders' confidence in the current problem-solving process is reassuring. As the anxiety of key individuals ebbs, the group problem-solving process can go forward.

3. They are curious.

The attitude of the scientist, an insatiable curiosity, drives him or her to find out how nature actually works. In order to find out the secrets of the universe, he or she formulates questions to study. Innate curiosity, if not completely squelched in formal schooling, can be a great asset to a leader. It helps design questions that, if answered, would take the group to where it wants to be. Going into a meeting with a few private questions for self about the emotional process of the group as well as the open question waiting to be resolved, can make for a most interesting and useful time.

This habit of asking questions is extremely useful in meetings. When statements are made that do not square with the principles of the group or with logic, the leader refrains from pointing out the deficiencies. Rather, becoming curious, he or she can interject a thoughtful question or two that will serve to get thinking back on course.

When the group seems to be stuck, the leader starts asking questions of himself or herself. Some of these thoughtful questions may go to the group. Along with theory as a guide they can greatly smooth the rocky road toward problem resolution.

When one white congregation refused their denominational support for black colleges, their minister did not lecture or preach at them. She asked a simple question: "Does anyone here know a black person?" This led to a lively creative discussion. It was decided to invite a black choir to sing. There were other exchanges. The donation situation was resolved shortly thereafter.

4. They observe.

Once a scientist formulates the questions, he or she gets answers by observing nature. In an organization, a leader, by simply observing, can learn how the emotional system works— where anxiety most frequently arises, how it circulates, how it escalates, how the group gets stuck, what leadership activity is useful, and what is not.

Further, when the leader's anxiety begins to rise, a conscious effort to go into "observation mode" can work wonders. An observer, say, Jane Goodall watching her chimps, does not blame, criticize, get angry with, distance from, boss, get dominated by, or dump her own anxiety onto them. She simply watches, making notes, seeing what she can learn. The time to define herself as a result of what she has learned, comes later. But she does not feel compelled to spell out to the chimps all she has learned about them.

Simply having an interested observer as a member of the group is most useful to the group emotional process, especially if the one observing is in a leadership position. The observer is, just by observing, already a little "out" of the group emotional process.

5. They define their thinking.

Extraordinary Leaders, though they do not push their ideas on the group, are not shy. Instead, they see problem-solving as an interactive process. If the group takes an active part in solving its own problems, from its best individual thinking, *it will be likely to own the solutions and implement them.*

The leader is an important part of the group in problem-solving, however. Seeing problems through the lens makes a difference, and thinking systems means that *he or she has important ideas to contribute.* The effective leader does not shrink from putting his or her way of thinking about the dilemma on the table.

The leader is neither married to his or her idea, nor averse to modifications that may be needed. He or she is open to discussion, interacting well and thinking clearly.

When a high level leader's ideas are presented, they are not given as commands or directives, but rather, in a way that conveys: "This is how I am looking at the question at present. What do you think?"

Let us go on to consider some more of their characteristics:

Facilitator and promoter of guiding principles

High level leaders, working over time for clarity on their own guiding principles, are familiar with their value. They know their benefits. They are the perfect ones to assist their groups to define their guiding principles.

Just as individuals with guiding principles do much better in life, organizations do as well. Just as principles are calming, grounding and orienting for individuals, they are for congregations also. So at some time, the congregation or organization will need to gain some clarity on just what those principles are.

Because thinking is done better as an individual, rather than as a group effort, the leader can facilitate the process by encouraging individual thinking in a variety of ways. Sometimes asking for written thoughts ahead of the meeting is useful. Addressing the chair rather than each other keeps group emotional process at a minimum. It is always easier for individuals to do their best thinking when group emotional process is less. But setting principles, for an individual is a solitary process. For a group, while individual thinking must be brought to the table, it must be eventually a contributive process, where many people contribute their thinking. In the end, the group will arrive at principles that, taken together, can serve as a compass for future thinking and action.

Extraordinary Leaders as well as other leadership in the group can refer to these for guidance, course correction, and to create new initiatives. *While setting principles is an interactive process in which the group participates, it is a leadership function to keep them in mind and keep externalizing them to the group.*

Leaders may also need to be aware when it is time to revisit them if new data are available that may, at some time, dictate revision.

Vision, mission, goal facilitator, and promoter

Based in a congregation's guiding principles, and consistent with them, comes formulation of the organization's mission, vision, and purpose. They translate the guiding principles into action terms. Its *mission* tells it why it is here—what it can do better than any other organization or congregation. Its *vision* is its best dream of where it hopes to go in the future. Its *goals* set out, as concretely as possible, steps for the short term realization (over the next few years) of mission and, ultimately, vision.

In the designing stages of these group guidelines, one has to keep in mind the leader's level on the scale, as well as that of the group. What are the facts of the system's resources? What about the leader's relationship with the rest of the group—how well is it working? How closely are these plans following the guiding principles? What might be dreamed up might not be possible, considering realistic limitations. At the same time, if limitations are overfocused, of course, nothing will be accomplished.

Again, individual thinking is emphasized and encouraged in every way possible, but once that is in place, an interactive process (with the leader) is needed to finally agree upon and adopt these guidelines.

One of the most important functions of the Extraordinary Leader is to be perfectly clear about mission, vision, and goals, bringing them to awareness often, especially in planning meetings, sermons, or talks, and in discussion with others, making them live. They may change more often than the basic guiding principles do. *Though the group creates its compass and*

131

guidebook, the leader must take responsibility for enunciating the vision, mission, and goals from time to time. The leader needs to see that they are not forgotten, but stay in awareness, energized and implemented.

Guiding principles and their outward expressions—vision, mission, and goals—are characteristics of high level leaders and groups. Thus, *as groups define for themselves what they believe, where they are going, and how they are going to get there, they gain in their functioning level.*

Of course, *if the leader does the solitary work of differentiating and defining self in all his or her own important systems the group will, in time, come up in functioning to meet the leader.*

Networkers with a wider perspective

High level individuals, in addition to working to improve their own nuclear family relationships, strive to get and maintain working relationships with as many people in their extended family as they can.

In the same way, the Extraordinary Leader stays in contact with the "extended family" of the organization—its conference, synod, hierarchy, or association. For leaders who came out of their families with an "authority problem" (in poor relationship with a parent), there may be an actual aversion to staying in contact with his or her superiors—the bishop, executive or association officers. To move toward becoming an Extraordinary Leader, however, relationships above as well as below, on social hierarchies, must be well tended. It is a perfect opportunity to work on any residual authority attitude, whatever patterned form it might take. Life will go better if leaders stay in touch with their leaders on a regular basis. If one's original parental relationships are addressed, the others are that much easier.

Another important function of Extraordinary Leaders is that of keeping contact with the wider world. A group can become isolated, cut off from its own community. When that happens, it is probably not sympathetic to human problems in the wider world or seeing much past its own congregation with any clarity. Sometimes, though, the group itself is so immersed in problems that it would be inappropriate to widen its scope until its own house is in better order.

The leader can sometimes broaden local vision by making contact with his or her clergy colleagues in the community. This can have a great effect on breaking the cut off pattern of a group. Once people start looking around them, they usually are energized to be responsible and responsive in local needs and issues. Though it is unlikely that any local group can solve the problems of the whole world, they can begin with addressing local issues to the extent possible.

Often, however, the leader has to set the pace and show a willingness to interact with community colleagues. It is only a small step from the neighborhood to the wider world.

Congregations today

In order to consider the special situations facing leaders in today's world, let us look at a few:

- How systems change with level of anxiety
- "Difficult people"
- Issues as anxiety markers
- Special cases
- Extraordinary Leaders respond

1. How systems change with level of anxiety

Contemporary society might be called "The Age of Anxiety." There are many triggers for anxiety in our world. If the presence of weapons of mass destruction are not enough, there is the fragile economy, the shrinking dollar, too much information, a loss of morals, decline of education, decline of the church, racial prejudice, business downsizings, reorganization, terrorism, immigration, and old age.

As society becomes anxious, systems within it respond in kind. *The anxious organization is a very different animal from what it is in calmer times.* Like the anxious individual, a group under the effects of anxiety can show a great deal of immature thinking and behavior.

Anxiety is automatic, it only needs to be triggered. When it rises, it is catching. Then, emotional intensity in relationships rise, and all the relationship patterns come out in full view. So when we see the relationship patterns, we can take it as a sign of rising or elevated anxiety. If, instead of getting involved in the anxious relationship patterns, we can look for the anxiety behind the patterns, addressing it, we'll be more effective.

What are some of the triggers for increased congregational anxiety?

- *A congregational nodal event.* Someone with an important functional position in the group has left it, or someone new has entered. This is particularly the case when a minister leaves and a new one comes.

- *Nodal events in families of the congregation.* These can increase their anxiety and spread throughout the rest of the group

- *Nodal events in the life of the leader.* As his or her anxiety increases, it will affect the rest of the congregation.

- *Community changes* such as a major corporation leaving or arriving (affecting jobs of people in the community or congregation or the general economy)

- *Unresolved anxiety originating among the leadership* of the group

- *Shrinking numbers* of the congregation (though this is more likely to be a symptom that can also act as an anxiety trigger) or the denomination

- *Unresolved anxiety in the denomination.* This can have to do with self-definition, money, shrinking numbers, or other important news.

An Extraordinary Leader, rather than criticizing the group for its patterns, will start looking for what the triggers behind the anxiety might be. When those are addressed, the anxiety will recede. But until they are, it will simply recycle, and break out in new forms. The calm connected leader, working on increasing his or her own level of differentiation makes a huge difference to the anxious organization, simply by keeping self on course. By reminding the group of its guiding principles, unique mission, vision for the future, and goals, the leader assists the group in quickly getting back on track.

2. "Difficult" people

At times of high anxiety in a group, some people will be even more "difficult" than usual, spilling their anxiety out into the group in unexpected ways. How do we think about them? How do we manage ourselves around them and the curve balls they throw? Sometimes they have already received a "diagnosis," which can prejudice our thoughts about and dealing with them.

Systems thinkers will try to ignore the diagnoses and blame, seeing them simply as barometers of the increased anxiety of the group or their families. The high level leader addresses them, in ways that reduces their anxiety rather than adding to it. Within limits, though one might wish they would act and react differently than they do, *"they are allowed."*[1] They arc simply doing what they do when anxious. The leader has choices. One does not have to take on their anxiety.

Addressing the anxiety behind their behavior, we can ask some questions. Are they experiencing nodal events or other anxiety triggers in their families? Are they simply responding to a higher than usual level of congregational anxiety? Have there been nodal events—someone coming into or leaving the congregation lately?

---

[1] This useful phrase was given to the author by colleague and long time systems thinker, Pat Meyer, several years ago.

Do limits ever have to be set? Sometimes, the immature, difficult people have to be reigned in. They may be going against the guiding principles of the group or outside the organizational guidelines. If the leader can make more frequent contact with difficult people (notwithstanding the fact that we all want to distance from them) they will often settle down. These contacts don't have to be large amounts of time, they simply need to take place. And, sometimes, they don't need to be about issues. Contact simply needs to be made.

Sometimes the immaturity, in the form of a small group, threatens to take over the congregation. Extraordinary Leaders, working with the more emotionally mature of the group in these cases, have seen wonderful success in setting limits in the name of the entire group. The leader is not alone in these cases. There is other leadership there, lay leaders or other staff members, waiting to assist or even to take the lead at times when needed. This kind of effort may take some time and thought, but it is worth it. The maturity of the group, initiated by the leader, can define itself to the immaturity in the same way high functioning parents lead in the best sense by defining themselves in their families from time to time.

3. Issues as Anxiety Markers

Just as difficult people and relationship patterns serve to show that anxiety is high, "issues" can be the same kind of a marker. It has often been said that the issue is not the issue. Sometimes it is. But often it is not. Often intense issues seem more important than they really are. They are simply signs that anxiety is rising in the group. If the leader takes issues as simply markers of anxiety, he or she can start to observe, be curious, and find out what is at the root of the anxiety. The group may or may not be aware of the actual trigger.

But if it can be dealt with, the "issues" will melt, giving way to solutions.

4. Special cases

Extraordinary Leaders find that they have fewer and fewer problems of the varieties we often see today, as they progress up the scale of differentiation.

Sexual harassment, often alleged, rarely if ever becomes an issue for leaders who are well aware of boundaries and live within them.

Gender, racial and other kinds of "prejudice," and "harassment" allegations don't arise when people are related to as equals. When the group does not treat some members as equals, the leader can, from principle, show a better way without telling anyone what to do.

What if one is working under immature leadership, or leadership that puts the immaturity in control or doesn't relate well with one over time? In those cases one may need to:

- With a great deal of thought, and hopefully, coaching, one needs to let one's superior know how one thinks about whatever is going on, using one's systems lens, being as open and transparent as possible, and how one plans to proceed.

- Try very hard to be in better touch with one's superior, improving the relationship.

- If those efforts fail over time and with substantial effort, then one may need to start looking for or request another place to serve.

5. Extraordinary Leaders respond to anxious systems.

Living in the midst of an anxious system (as most leaders today do) is an opportunity to pull up one's level of functioning.

Whenever one pulls up in functioning, the group will react, temporarily, in a negative way. However, if the leader maintains good contact with other leadership in the group, staying in touch with angles of triangles, (especially the most anxious ones) the group calms down and joins the leader at a new, higher level of functioning.

The leader's watchwords during times of high anxiety are:

- Observing, listening, being curious,
- Managing self, not taking on the anxiety,
- Keeping in contact,
- Thinking systems, defining self factually, with logic and principles.

The thinking leader can see patterns in the group as well as his or her own position within it. From that vantage point one is in a position to plan next steps.

Extraordinary Leaders, defining self through the lens of systems theory and other life principles, becomes a tremendous resource for the anxious system.

Thinking It Over

Extraordinary Leaders, in anxious times with their anxious systems, may find themselves in some rather intense and trying situations. Looking at situations and managing self through the lens of Bowen family systems theory will point the way to function in a way that is useful to self and to the group. Ideally, special situations will be an occasion for stepping up in one's personal life functioning.

Real Life Research

1. What are some of the characteristics of Extraordinary Leaders as they interact with their systems?

2. Describe a relationship master.

3. Describe how Extraordinary Leaders go about problem-solving

4. Have you been in a group that had this kind of leader?

5. What is leadership's responsibility where vision, mission and goals are concerned?

6. Why are the guiding principles of an organization important?

7. How do guiding principles relate to organizational tasks of question 5?

8. How does a systems thinker look at "difficult" people?

9. How much choice do you have in an anxious environment, to stay out of the anxiety?

10. What are some anxiety triggers you are aware of that might be operating in your family, congregation, denomination, or faith at present?

10

Clergy Counseling

When they are at the end of the rope, unable to think clearly
and not knowing where to turn, a very large number of people go
first to a minister, priest, or rabbi. This fact sets the profession
apart from others. Some clergy people have some training in
consulting with people in these situations, but many do not. If
they have received any training at all, it is usually based in "old
(traditional) theory," seeing the individual as the emotional unit
rather than the family. They are thinking "cause and effect"
rather than thinking systems. They often see someone as being
"to blame." In that case, lacking neutrality, they may actually
add to the problem. Or, getting into an "advisor" role with which
they are more comfortable, they may feel they have to have the
answer, not understanding the value of listening, being curious,
trying to simply understand.

What can be accomplished in three sessions?

Many clergy people are constrained by their organizations to
limit their counseling to three sessions. Some are "allowed" (or
allow themselves) a few more sessions, and some are
uncomfortable with even three.

But even in three sessions, one can, thinking systems, be of great usefulness to a family or an individual. Since the clergy stand in such an important place for people with problems, they need the best thinking available. Counseling can assist people to find solutions to situations and resolution for anxiety.

If, however, after three sessions, there seems to be no resolution, one can certainly make a referral. A list of Bowen theory trained coaches in one's area is invaluable (Someone at one of the centers listed in Appendix III can assist.)

One cannot but wonder: if more clergy people knew Bowen theory, would there be less divorce? How many families would be how much better off? Would all of society itself be the beneficiary?

Where does the clergy counselor focus?

All Bowen theory-based coaches try to maintain a primary focus on managing themselves well when relating to others. They try primarily not to take on the anxiety of others, connect thoughtfully with them and to show how theory guides in life situations. This ability is based on their work on self in family relationships. *One can only be as effective as one is in family relationships.* The calm, connected, groundedness one gains in working on his or her own family relationships will carry over to the consulting room just as it does in other roles.

If one is 51% focused on managing self in consulting (and in all of life), it still leaves 49% to listen and think how theory applies.

The Coaching Process

Some of the most important parts of the coaching process, for systems-thinking coaches, are:

- Calming of anxiety
- Connecting with the family emotional system
- Observing

- Managing self, not trying to change others
- Defining self through the lens of theory

1. Calming anxiety.

The first goal in consulting is anxiety reduction. If people are intensely anxious, their thinking becomes unreliable. When the anxiety decreases, they can think. Often they can think their way through to resolution. Their solutions or resolutions may not be those of the consultant. They may be better than anything he or she could have come up with.

How do we calm anxiety? It doesn't happen by telling people to be calm. Rather, there are at least three ways one can be a calming influence on self and the system. The most important way to lower the emotional intensity in the consulting room is *for the consultant to be calm.* This does not mean to fake being calm, but to really be, inside, emotionally calm. How does one get calm and un-anxious, especially when the emotional field in the room is all stirred up? People have a variety of ways to calm their emotional brains. Some swear by taking deep breaths and "exhaling the anxiety." The author most efficiently gets to a calm state by becoming the observer. *Simply watching, as does the scientist, out of intellectual curiosity, works a kind of magic.* Anxiety disappears.

Secondly, when there is more than one person in the room, we structure the session by *asking people to speak only to the coach, not speaking to each other, taking turns and not interrupting each other.* This may be difficult for some families to follow in the beginning. *But it has the effect of keeping the group emotional process from escalating beyond the capacity of the thinking brain to function reliably.* Careful thinking is what brings people to resolution of life problems, not, as traditional theory has taught us, venting emotion.

Lastly, the coach works to continue *to guide the process toward thinking* and thoughtful management of self. He or she demonstrates an important life attitude, by continuing to be curious and factual, bringing logic and theory to bear. *As people*

143

get to the thinking parts of their brains, they automatically become emotionally less intense. The cerebral cortex inhibits the emotional centers of the brain. So, the more one thinks, the more one is able to think. Then, solutions and resolution begin to emerge. They are implemented, though, not in the consultation office but in the family emotional field.

Life difficulties are not resolved and people do not go up in functioning by the emotional unloading they may have been trained to do by other "therapy" experiences. *A more permanent and reliable result is obtained by thinking than by venting.*

2. Connecting with the family emotional system.

The coach's connecting intellectually to the emotionality that a family is bringing is experienced as helpful and useful by the family.

The coach accomplishes this, usually, by *asking questions.* These are not considered impolite, or "prying" in the consulting room, especially if the coach is gentle and respectful. Being curious and trying to get the whole picture is expected in a coaching setting. If the questions are based on systems thinking they will be useful and assist to better functioning, since they are emotionally neutral, don't imply blame and don't take sides. These kinds of questions assist people to clarify their thinking.

Not having the answers is a foreign concept to most people in the helping professions such as the ministry. But it is very helpful to people in a consulting room. *Actually, none of us does have the answers for another life or family.* Biting the tongue when we're tempted to tell other people what to do, how to fix it, or what next steps to take, is most useful in assisting them to get to their own answers. Confidence in individuals' and families' abilities to figure things out will encourage them to work toward resolution. Moreover, when they create their own answer they are more likely to remember and implement it than when we "lay it on" them.

How many family members need to be present in order to be doing "family counseling"? Since the family is an emotional unit, there is a sense in which, if only one is in the room, the whole family is there. What affects one affects the entire unit. So if one person in the family begins to do better there will be a positive effect on the rest of the group, if they are in contact with each other. Whoever is motivated to be present and work on self will break ground for the whole system. One does not need more than one person to think systems or assist from a family theory perspective.

Of course, the more of the family the coach meets, the better his or her understanding of the whole unit.

Often parents earnestly desire us to take their teenagers and fix them, wake them up or otherwise transform them. What they are really wanting is for us to do their work for them. We will usually fail miserably at this assignment. But, *since parents are the best coaches for children,* with some coaching from a family systems theory base and encouragement, they can usually do a better job than any of us could presume to do with someone else's children. *If we take over the job for them it says to them that they were right—they weren't adequate parents.* That is a judgmental, overfunctioning, minimizing posture.

Also, if parents will get their marital relationship in better working order, (more open, equal and separate) most often the children's difficulties will dissolve, over time.[1]

3. Observing systems.

One of the best ways for a coach to connect without giving advice is to simply observe. When Bowen worked on bringing the study of the human into the realm of science, he began by simply observing families in formal research. He found that the research families did better than other families he was seeing. There is a potent effect to be had from simply observing what is going on through the lens of theory. Just watching, calms self and any system one is connected with.

---

[1] See Gilbert, M., *Connecting With Our Children,* Wiley and Sons, New York, 1999, for greater detail on this subject.

Observing, with its wonderful ability to calm the emotional centers of the brain, actually produces relaxation, objectivity, and a quick way to get to constructive thinking.

4. Coach manages self.

The coach manages self, not the others. It is paradoxical that people who need help, get more assistance from someone who can refrain from helping, staying out of their emotional field, emotionally, *yet connect with it intellectually.*

Observing is part of managing self, since, as we have seen, it is calming.

Continuing to think, though the person or family in the room may be emotionally intense, can be a challenge. But thinking promotes thinking by inhibiting emotional centers. So as we continue to think, the anxiety lowers in self.

As people converse with another calmer self, they become calmer. Calm is catching, as is anxiety, though it happens slower.

5. Defining self, "through the lens."

The coach is not a passive observer. At some time, the coach will define "through the lens of theory," how he or she sees the dilemmas that have been brought in. Concepts, principles or ideas from theory, and how they apply, are explained. If these are guiding principles for the coach, they will have their calming, organizing effect on all in the room—including the coach!

Defining theory in each session is a teaching moment. It is often fairly brief, and is not a lecture. It is as close to having answers as we get. *Theory itself is the answer to the human relationship impasses* that are brought into the consulting room. Many people become interested in reading more or watching tapes or DVDs on Bowen family system theory. This facilitates the process—the faster people learn theory, the more they can use it. The theoretical ideas themselves will point the way to answers.

Know theory, know theory, know theory. If you know it you can use it. If you don't, you can't.

6. When and where to refer for further coaching.

There are several guidelines for recommending further assistance. A referral should be made if:

- The person or family needs more than the number of sessions one can or wants to, give,
- Someone may get hurt, or
- The person or family is asking for a referral.

If the couple or person is going to need more than the number of sessions one is prepared to give, refer them.

If someone may get hurt, refer them. Suicide or homicidal threats are to be taken seriously. They are an emergency. These must be asked about if people appear depressed, withdrawn or angry. If the answer is positive, they should be referred to the nearest emergency room (with suicidal ideas or threats) or police station (if homicidal ideas are present). Police can determine if psychiatric care is indicated. These numbers should be readily availably at the desk of anyone who does any amount of counseling.

If people want a referral, give it. The list of centers in this book may help. The people listed may know someone to recommend in the local area even if they themselves are not close by.

Be selective in choosing a coach, for self or for others, if at all possible. *Many who call themselves "family systems oriented" have had little or no training or experience with coaching for themselves.* And, if there is no family systems coach, but one knows a local person to be sensitive, respectful and competent, he or she may be a useful resource as well.

How the counselor thinks: the lens.

The longer one thinks systems the better one becomes at it. It really is a different way of conceptualizing the human. Seeing the family as the emotional unit is not the way we ordinarily think. So, training and continued exposure to the ideas, over as long a term as possible, is mandatory for anyone wanting to do counseling from the systems theory perspective.

From knowledge of human and natural emotional systems, the coach thinks about such issues as anxiety level and its important place in an emotional system. Relationship patterns are observed and explained. The issue may or may not be the issue. And everything looks very different once the anxiety level lowers.

An understanding of the scale of differentiation of self challenges the coach to be always working on stepping up in his or her own functioning. It will show coach and consultees what the "next step up" in functioning is. Working on differentiation is not limited by age, culture or diagnosis. Whereas traditional theory was thought to be applicable only to fairly young age groups, differentiation of self is pushed by people of all ages and optimally, for the rest of their lives. It applies to all cultures, since humans of all cultures are more alike than they are different. Emotionally, they are the same.

Diagnosis is not a deterrent to differentiation. In fact the coach does not work from diagnoses, but rather from thinking about functioning and stepping up.

Though the clergy counselor may not be engaging a family over the years of time needed for differentiation (though some do, when they have the training), thinking can be informed by the scale. It can certainly challenge one's own performance.

How to become a counselor.

The following are some of the most important ways for the clergy counselor to prepare for his or her important job of counseling informed by Bowen family system theory.

"Know theory, know theory, know theory." Theory so informs work in Bowen family systems counseling that a basic, grounded knowledge, with all the elements of didactic training, reading, writing and personal coaching, with continuing exposure to the ideas is essential. What helps, in this way of working, is theory itself—a more accurate, useful way of seeing. It is not the

relationship with the counselor that leads to long term benefit. It is not "dumping" anxiety that provides solutions. To the extent that theory is taken in, and made use of, there will be more solid gains, not simply of a quick, "feel good" fix that does not last. So the counselor, in order to think systems in intense situations, must be well-grounded in theoretical training and practical use of theory that includes case load supervision.

Work on becoming more of a self in one's own family is another essential to the development of anyone who consults based on Bowen theory. Just as working on family relationships has a wonderful effect on leadership abilities and capacity, it has the same effect in one's counseling efforts. As one becomes more separate, open and equal with those challenging people called family, it happens in all arenas, including in the consulting room. One learns a great deal about coaching from his or her experience with personal coaching.

Because *thinking systems may not square with other counseling* people have experienced or with what the culture propounds, the counselor has to develop a certain amount of comfort with being different. He or she may have to define that this may be different, but has been useful to many. Other professionals have questioned the author about certain practices: for example seeing people every two weeks instead of weekly. People may have been "trained" by past counseling experience, to intensely emote in the session. We know this will interfere with thinking and resolution, so some "retraining" or explaining may be needed. If one is comfortable with being different and thinking differently one can relate to these and the many other questions that arise from having "a new way of thinking" without becoming defensive.

Techniques—what the counselor does.

To briefly review what happens in counseling: theory leads the way, but some useful techniques for counseling grow out of its ideas:

- Decreasing emotional process,

- Managing self emotionally,
- Defining self.

Managing emotional process in the room.

One of the most useful "how-to's" is, when there is more than one person in the consultation, asking people to speak only to the coach and not to each other.

Many couples, under these circumstances, can actually listen to each other, when they cannot at home, because of the escalation that takes place when they try to interact. They often comment about the usefulness of this structure for becoming more objective and neutral. They talk of understanding their spouses in a new way. After they get used to it, most people see the utility of this way of proceeding. They gladly observe its constraints. They often express gratitude for it.

The coach's managing self emotionally is most useful to people coming for assistance. It means that all can think better, remembering theory. It also means one can stay more neutral, not taking sides, but rather seeing how each person contributes to their mutual difficulty.

Defining self is not telling people what to do or what to think. It merely says, "This is how I see it." It brings concepts of theory into the room. People cannot know too much Bowen theory. But in the consulting room, where there are teaching moments, we are not in a classroom. It has to be given in small doses.

The importance of counseling that "thinks systems."

By now, several thousand families have benefited from the guidance of coaches who are systems thinkers. They attest to the real changes they have been able to sustain. Individuals have benefited as well as families. Now, as family systems theory goes into organizations such as congregations, there may ultimately be an observable positive effect on society itself.

Would society be different?

Prevailing, individual, cause and effect, traditional theory, is by now a part of our society and people lead their lives by it. While it may have had limited usefulness to some, in many ways it has been devastating. It may have even facilitated the regressive spiral we now find ourselves in. One wonders how things might have been different if the helping professions had been given Bowen theory in the beginning.

One presumes that personal responsibility would have been more a part of the ethos of the culture rather than "the pleasure principle" of Freud, to which our society seems so dedicated at present. If permissive childrearing had not become the norm, would we have as many children having children? Would families in general have fared better if the cutoff aspect of divorce were better understood and if they had had a way to think about working toward resolution of their difficulties?

Leaders would have useful, helpful guidelines that work. We as a society might have actually produced more high level leaders.

Thinking It Over

Bowen theory stands in contradistinction to traditional theory used most in the counseling professions. It sees the family, rather than the individual as the emotional unit. This bigger picture of the human opens the way for systems thinking and other concepts that derive from it. It works to lower anxiety, increase responsibility for self management and often is able to preserve family units, guiding them to better functioning.

Real Life Research

1. What differences are there in counseling from a traditional rather than a Bowen theory perspective?

2. What is the main job of the counselor in the consulting room? What facilitates that coming about?

3. How many people have to be present in the room to do family counseling? Why?

4. Why are coaches usually unsuccessful with children and adolescents? Who are the best coaches for them?

5. When is further counseling needed?

6. Do you prefer to limit the number of sessions you do with consultees? Are you clear on your boundaries in counseling?

7. Why is it necessary to know theory in order to do counseling?

8. What kind of preparation does a counselor need?

9. Why is thinking stressed in Bowen theory based counseling?

10. How might society be different if Bowen theory were accepted as guiding principle rather than traditional theory?

11

On the Importance of the Clergy

There is no profession like that of the minister or rabbi, that has as one of its missions to walk alongside families, celebrating, mourning, worshipping with them. The clergy help us all bring special meaning and memories to the milestones in life, endowing them—and thus all of life—with significance that can be attained in no other way. By asking God's blessing on these tremendously important events, clergy people help us affirm the central transcendent, spiritual value we sense and hope for in human existence.[1]

Clergy people, in most cases, preside over a weekly meeting of people who receive no credit and get no pay for being there. In fact they are usually given responsibilities—their time, effort and money are needed. They come, as Dr. Ammerman discovered in her research, to hear about God.[2] And they apparently see this pursuit as very important—they keep coming. They come to church over years and generations of time, to

---

[1] This chapter was inspired by the author's attending the funeral of a friend and seeing how the family responded to their clergy friend, Rev. William Nabers, and he to them, as he entered the sanctuary.

[2] See chapter 2 for a fuller explanation of this research.

worship, to learn, to be baptized, confirmed, married, and buried. But, they come, mostly, to hear about God.

We humans seem to need to find God,[3] or else this phenomenon of church would have died long ago. Certainly there have been attempts to kill it. But it lives on, all over the world.[4] The clergy bring news we want to hear, teaching us how to live, love, and die, staying beside us throughout life in a vital way that no other profession does.

Let us walk through eight of the myriad functions of ministry, thinking systems as we go:

- Benefits of being a part of a congregation
- The weekly service
- Weddings
- Christening, dedication, baptism
- Teaching
- Visiting the sick
- Funerals
- Community outreach

1. Benefits of being part of a congregation

As we have seen, by simply gathering on a regular basis, a congregation of believers forms an emotional unit—a system, with all of its advantages as well as its drawbacks. The congregation can be of tremendous support to each other at times of nodal events in individuals' and families' lives. It can be a life line for those with special needs. It can make a tremendous

---

[3] Dr. Joanne Bowen, anthropologist, reiterated the well know fact that there are no known societies without religion, in a lecture at the Bowen Center for the Study of the Family in 2003.
[4] In Europe, where church-going is said to be dying, the author found at least one church in Austria, a small cathedral, open and vibrant on Sunday morning. European friends say they still join churches, marry there and are buried there.

difference for service in communities. At best, life is difficult, but being a part of a congregation can ease the way significantly.

The clergy leader can facilitate the congregation's best functioning simply by knowing the importance of women's groups, the choir, and pot luck dinners. The leader who discounts congregational subgroups and social functions, doesn't understand emotional systems.

2. The weekly service

Out of the daily humdrum of our lives we gather, taking time out to celebrate and affirm life and belief, as people have for thousands of years—to pray, to connect with each other, to sing, to read the sacred writings, to learn, to repeat the rituals—to find God.

Science, long disinterested in things religious, is accumulating evidence that going to church or synagogue is good for health (physical, mental/emotional, and social), for the strength of the family and marriage and for the rearing of children. Church-going families rear fewer delinquents and fewer addicts. Church-going children are more involved in socially positive community activities.[5]

The rituals of religion[6] may be a necessary part of religious observance, since our reptilian brain craves repetition. (Even denominations who say they eschew ritual seem to do things the same way, week after week.) Music, art, costume all appeal to the emotional or limbic part of the brain, stimulating the mood. Readings and the sermon, involve the thinking, cerebral brain, stirring us to think about what it is we believe and how we act in community and in society. Thus, all of the triune brain is involved in the worship service.

---

[5] As emphasized in M. Scott Peck's *The Road Less Traveled,* Touchstone, New York, 1978.
[6] Look through the *Handbook of Religion and Health,* by Koenig et.al. Oxford U. Press, 2001 to see the results of over 1,000 research studies on these subjects compiled into one volume.

In the sermon, Extraordinary Leaders have a chance to take the time to get clear on something, thinking it all the way through for themselves, seeing what they believe and then defining it to a group. If they preach about what they themselves are clear about—not merely what they were taught in seminary—they are coming from basic self and people find it fascinating. It is a uniquely human activity. (One never sees other species sitting around in a group, listening to a leader.) But the fascination with the best leaders is not when they tell us what to do, how to think or feel. It is when they define themselves— what it is they think. It is an "I Position." There is some time to explain, support and elaborate on the position, but the interesting and compelling phenomenon of the best sermons is their ability to say, human to human (in an equal posture with the listeners) what and how one thinks about a given subject.

Praying together may be an important aspect of why people attend church. In certain people prayer has been observed to change brain waves from anxious to calm and observing—the kind we would all like to have, but sometimes takes years of training to develop.[7]

3. Weddings

What is the best way to prepare people for marriage? Does anyone know? Extensive course-work, elaborate tests to see if the marriage will work or if people are compatible and sometimes group activities are prescribed. What would be a family systems theory way of going?

Some family systems oriented premarital counseling has helped those attending to construct a family diagram, with as many people as they know of, or can find out about, represented. The couples are then sent out to meet as many of the people on the diagram as possible, then return and report on whom they met and what they learned about their family. This is sound from a theoretical standpoint, since:

---

[7] Discovered in pilot research by Victoria Harrison. Her paper on the subject can be obtained from www.hsystems.org.

- How much formal teaching is actually heard, anyway, by people in the emotionally intense glow just before they marry?

- Connecting with extended family is emotionally grounding—it is a life-stabilizing force for those who take it seriously, continuing the connecting. Marriage needs all the stabilizing it can get at present.

- It provides a wonderful opportunity to teach about the emotional and functioning liabilities involved in cutoff, proposing principles for family life into the future.

Wedding ceremonies today are as varied as can possibly be imagined. The variation means that they have the possibility of being quite personalized. In the end, they are an important defining of selves before God, family and the world, the celebration of the beginning of a new family. The clergy's officiating part in the process endears them to families and the families to them, sometimes for a lifetime.

Bowen called someone entering or leaving a family a "nodal event." These events mean that all the triangles are re-formed to some extent. To an extent they remain in place. To some degree, two people are leaving their respective nests. Also, two extended families are receiving new members. With so many nodal events going on in two families at once, it is easy to see why there is both crying and rejoicing at weddings! It will take some time before the jostling of the triangles in the family can be accommodated.

Family members find family ceremonies a wonderful time to reconnect with members that may have been somewhat out of connection. For systems thinkers, they are not-to-be-missed occasions.

4. Christening, baptism or dedication of children

Birth, when a new life enters the family, is a nodal event of major importance, rearranging the triangles significantly. And with each subsequent birth, the number of potential triangles increases tremendously.

The church's contribution to solemnizing the entrance of a baby or young person into the family and into the congregation cannot be overestimated. The welcoming ceremony of the church is also a dedication of the parents and church to the spiritual training of the child.

All of this is reassuring and calming to the family at the anxious times that nodal events represent, especially in today's anxious world. The nodal events of especially intense families— their births, deaths and marriages—can generate enough anxiety to spill into the congregation.

Some churches are beginning to conduct parent training classes as a service to strengthen families. Family systems theory, with its directives can point the way for better family functioning in such training. Parents' awareness of how to connect with each other and then their children, without over-focusing (smothering) on the one hand, or neglecting on the other, can be as useful for them as leadership training in systems thinking is for the clergy.

5. Teaching

An active congregation is always a learning group, wanting to know more. Some may be actually working on their guiding principles. Whether in Sunday School, new congregant classes, preparation for confirmation or bar or bat mitzvah, or study of the Bible, teaching is always an important function of the church or synagogue. Family systems theory does not tell us what to teach. It does spell out something about the process of teaching and learning:

- The emotional posture of the teacher is important.
- Whether learners are taught or think it through makes a life long difference.

The emotional posture of the teacher. If the teacher maintains an equal posture with the learners, they are much more apt to take an active part in the process, the only way they can absorb the material. From what we have seen about the patterns, we know that if the teacher is dictatorial or over authoritarian, (an overfunction) the learner will become anxious, unable to think well and thus left with a diminished ability to learn because the cerebral cortex will be flooded with anxiety.

If the teacher adopts an underfunctioning posture, being unsure, putting the learners in charge of the structure, they again will be anxious, not comfortable in that position. They may take over, and "teach" much that is not intended. An unfocused process may be the result.

Of course, openness is what teachers are aiming for, though it is best structured in order to keep group emotional process at bay.

The teacher's own boundaries and amount of basic self are always apparent. In the best situation, teaching is done out of basic self, the teacher having thought through and adopted for self what he or she is teaching. That kind of teaching is anything but dull—it is attractive and fascinating to the learners.

Are we teaching a thinking-through process? If the goal of a class is to simply get through the material as it is in a book, the learning will not be memorable or remembered. If the goal of teaching is to inspire learners to think information through, then, to the extent they do that, it has the possibility of becoming part of their guiding principles for living.

How useful it would be if teachers were able to address this difference—being exposed to ideas as different from making them a part of life. What if teachers actually spelled out the process involved in adopting guiding principles? What if they actually challenged people in classes to think things through and come up with guiding principles for living? What if they asked more questions? How would the church be different? How would our communities benefit?

6. Visiting the sick

Clergy people take visiting the sick very seriously, though it requires a lot of effort, plays havoc with their schedules and can be depressing.

What can thinking systems contribute to this aspect of ministry? A few guidelines may be derived:

- Empathy (feeling the feelings of the person and family) can be a good thing, but brief doses by the leader are less draining to him or her, and more useful to the patient and the family. The quiet, calm, respectful—even objective—presence that listens in an understanding way, bringing his or her message of hope is what is really needed, even more than empathy, as many families have confirmed. *Understanding* may be a better goal.

- Prayer, with its advantageous brain state may be healing.

- The family of a desperately ill person may need ministry as much as the patient. This ministry, can ultimately, benefit the patient, since they are, in the same emotional unit.

- Listening and bearing with the questions and ability to be comfortable with not knowing can be more helpful than pat answers to the "Why me?" dilemmas.

- Congregational support at this time in all the wonderful forms it can take, is part of the definition of a high functioning group.

7. Death in the family

When life is ending, the family systems perspective is also useful. Much has been written on the subject of death and dying from the point of view of traditional theory, with its typical and even obligatory, stages at the end of life and of mourning.

Bowen wrote and lectured on the subject, pointing out:[8]

- *Open family systems*, who discuss grave diagnoses and the possibility or reality of dying honestly and clearly, do better than those who cannot or do not.

- *Expressing emotions* at the beginning is preferred to having them go underground in the system, circulating through it, wreaking havoc later.

- *Children* don't need to be "protected" from death.

- An *emotional "shock wave"* usually unrecognized by the family, can follow the death of a person important to the functioning of the family. It can reverberate through the generations of family members for years, with illnesses, divorce, accidents or behavior problems as symptoms.

- *Families can and do go on* after an important death.

- *All deaths are not equal*. While some are devastating, setting off shock waves, some are of little impact. Still others are a relief to the family emotional system.

The clergy person, by speaking openly of death with family members, can, like a physician, greatly facilitate the opening of a family system around nodal events such as grave illness, dying or death.

The author has noted the importance of family cutoff surrounding some deaths. In one family with teenagers, when the husband died, the wife did an amazing job of continuing on afterwards, though the death was anything but a relief. It seemed that the wife's staying connected with her dead spouse's family, avoiding cutoff with his extended family system, was the secret of her high functioning.[9] Other adults, who lost a parent young, and then were cut off from that family by the surviving parent,

---

[8] Bowen, *Family Therapy*, op. cit., p. 321.
[9] See Gilbert, R., *Connecting With Our Children,* op. cit., p.168, for a fuller explanation of this.

find a positive emotional response within themselves that can be more corrective than years of therapy, simply by connecting on a continuing basis with the dead parent's family.

A conclusion of work in this area is that the traditional "stages" of mourning and death cited by Kubler-Ross and others, (taken from Freud's writing), may *not* have to inevitably follow a death in the family. If there is an extended family of the dead person available to be connected with, it is extremely important to keep those connections in place. *The family is an emotional unit. Though the dead person is missed, the emotional process of the family from which he or she came, is most often still alive and available for connection. By staying connected with that live emotional process, cutoff and all its attendant negative effects are avoided.* Cutoff, the author has come to believe, is more from an emotional unit than from any particular part of it. That can be avoided. What Kubler-Ross may have described is not so much the effects of a death itself as the effects of cutoff that so often follows a death in a family.

Sometimes families become conflictual with each other and cut off around the time of a death. While issues are blamed for the cutoff, the family systems perspective would emphasize the underlying family process around such cutoffs more than any supposed "issues." Extraordinary Leaders are often in the significant position of sensing an impending cutoff in a family. They can point out the dire effects of cutoff and how much more pivotal are well-working family relationships to life functioning than had been imagined. In addition, they can underscore, if appropriate:

- The importance of as many extended family members connecting around the time of a death as possible,

- The need for family members to personalize the memory of the dead person at the service, and

- It can be a good release to cry.

The funeral service, like the wedding, has become varied and extremely personal to each family. What a wonderful, useful trend. It assists the family to;

- Say good-bye to the person,
- Celebrate the life of the person, remembering the poignant and powerful stories,
- Be there for each other at an important time in the life of the family,
- Make contact with distant family members,
- Go on with life and living, and
- Consider their spiritual beliefs.

All in all, no profession is as intimately connected with meaningful times in the lives of individuals and families, as is the clergy. In the last few generations, there has been an attempt to place in their stead, as "priests," the therapy profession. It didn't work. Many are realizing that therapy, while useful, cannot ever take the place of religious life or spirituality.

8. Community outreach and missions

Typical of church groups that are not stagnant or dying, is their desire to reach out with assistance for community needs. Some of the many projects that congregations with the leadership of their clergy have undertaken include: homeless shelters, after school care, Mom's day out programs, drug prevention and rehabilitation programs, outreach to gang members, athletic programs, holiday food donations to families, school supply and clothing donations, medical supplies to missions, disaster relief missions, teenage missions to other countries, food for hungry people programs, meals on wheels, and probably thousands of others. Those involved in disaster relief in the Gulf area report that there is a great number of vans, buses, trucks, and other assorted vehicles in the area, the great majority identified as belonging to a church or religious group.[10] What, indeed, would happen if churches were to suddenly stop being involved in the needs of their communities and the world?

Starting to care about the needs of the community outside the immediate congregation is a wonderful way for a group to get out of a distant, shut-down or cut off posture. Giving is life-giving. *It is never overfunctioning when assistance is needed!* In overfunctioning/underfunctioning, one person ends up anxious and minimized. But when needed help is given, both the helper as well as the helped feel good, gaining energy.

It is conceivable, as Dr. Menninger believed, that the clergy can lead us out of the societal regression in which we now find ourselves. If they take that direction, they will find the family systems perspective an enormous advantage.

Thinking It Over

The clergy's import to society cannot be overestimated. They are a calming, thinking influence who assist us to find spiritual meaning in life. Their importance to society and their potential for leadership in society is only dimly understood. Family systems theory can provide useful guidance for their relating as well as their wide and varied aspects of ministry.

Real Life Research

1. How are clergy unique in society?

2. What is the most important part of the weekly service? Why?

---

[10] The author's brother, Steve Gilbert, gave this first-hand report.

3. How difficult is it to stay out of the emotional field, yet connected, in visiting the sick or when someone has died? Why is it important to do?

4. What are nodal events? Why are they important to the system?

5. What emotional effects do nodal events have on a family?

6. How does the church assist families in nodal events?

7. Why are the Kubler-Ross stages of death and dying not inevitable?

8. What is an emotional shock wave?

9. What are characteristics of an open system? How can a clergy person assist a family system to open up?

10. What is cutoff and how does it come into play at times of nodal events?

11. What are goals for teaching in the congregational setting?

12. How can these goals be promoted?

12

Clergy Thinking Systems—Theory Confirmed

When the Extraordinary Leadership Seminar began several years ago, it was entered into in the spirit of adventure. A denomination's invitation was interesting. Where would it go? What would one teach? What would the clergy teach us? Adventure is also experiment, with more questions than answers.

At this point, the adventure continues—both in learning and in teaching. Some aspects of leadership have become clearer and more defined, however. They apply not only to clergy, but to all who find themselves in a position of leadership. The following points, which occur over and over in discussion periods and in coaching sessions, have served to confirm theory. They emerge as *hedges against pitfalls*. They are worth listing and then elaborating in more detail. Most have appeared earlier in the book but are repeated because of their importance.

- Take time for staff relationships.
- Stay in touch with your family system.
- Manage emotional process, especially in meetings.
- Don't be afraid to say "no" to the immaturity.
- One's emotional tone can be chosen.

- In a regression, one may be different.
- Be a Relationship Master, relating out of basic self, not pseudoself.

1. Take time for staff relationships.

Staff relationships are not a marriage, though they are often likened to one. It is easy to see which staff members spend a certain amount of time together and because of that, *do form an emotional system.* In a family, spouses or other members who do not spend enough time together have a distant relationship. Distance, one of the patterns, creates anxiety of its own that affects the entire system with increasing patterns and symptoms.

In the same way, *if staff members and church leadership do not spend an appropriate amount of time with each other, their relationships become distant, creating anxiety that will impair their own performance, propagating itself through the rest of the congregation.*

Rev. D, an associate minister was unhappy that his senior pastor was constantly undermining and sniping at him in various ways. Rev. D's work had only been superior and enhanced the congregation's functioning in every way. He did not understand what was triggering the negative attitude from his superior. The more he tried to please his boss, the more criticism he got. However, the two never sat down together to go over things or be on the same page. Rev. D, from his growing knowledge of systems theory, asked for a weekly time with the senior pastor to do just that. During the sessions, he tried to work on being equal (keeping his thinking going) though respectful of his boss's position (mindful of boundaries). He was open, bringing up everything he needed to, not venting, but staying to task reporting and clarification, guided by the mission, goals and purposes of the group. He found shortly after the sessions began that the negative attitude of his superior minister diminished. Before long, they were functioning as a well-working team.

Because the ministry is so demanding, it is tempting to go off on one's own, not making time for staff relationships. If it happens, the organization will malfunction just as a family will when two parents take too little time for each other. It is not enough to call a weekly staff meeting and think the relationships will work. *The leader needs to create one-on-one time for each staff member—alone, unrushed, on a regular basis, focused and attentive, if the relationships are to be what the organization needs from the leadership.* In addition, similar meetings with lay leaders on a regular basis will prevent a great deal of difficulty.

2. Stay in contact with your family system.

We have seen how we bring patterns and postures from our years in our families into our adult relationship functioning. We have seen the importance of taking these back to the family where they originated and working to lessen the negative patterns. Sometimes people make an initial effort with extended family relationships, doing genealogy, making trips to meet people and then think their family work is done!

Unfortunately, *working to become a better version of oneself is a never-ending proposition.* It is, at any rate, for those who aspire to constantly build more basic self, going higher on the scale. When people do what it takes to stay in better contact with their family of origin, they find they function better in life, carrying with them a more emotionally grounded steadiness.

Pastor L was dismayed that his retired parents would soon be moving into his town. They were not the calmest people in the world and sometimes, visits back home to work on himself had been a bit intense. The positive side of the move, however, was that their being closer would afford him an opportunity to do more of the work he knew he needed to do for self, to get a little more separate from the system. He, a youngest, would be able to step up to the plate of being an even more responsible son. He cheered himself that they would not be living with him and his family. They would be in their own residence some miles away. That distance might actually make their living close by, easier than the family visits where he would live with them a few days at a time.

Once, before a potentially intense board meeting was due, (during these it was usual for him to experience a panicky intensity inside that he did not like) he was at their home for a casual visit. He noticed later, at the meeting that he was calmer, more focused and composed than usual. The inner negative feeling had been gone. The meeting went quite well. He wondered if the visit with his family before the meeting was connected with this outcome for him.

To test this out, he began to plan short visits with his parents before every board meeting. The board meetings continued to find him calm, collected and lacking the usual inner anxiety he had become used to. He created ways to define himself during these meetings and found it easier than ever before to address emotional process when necessary, subtly but effectively.

Of course, this is not a prescription nor a recipe. It would not work for some to visit their families before intense working meetings as it did for Rev. L. For some, this formula would have the opposite effect. But the general theoretical principle holds true for all of us, *that if we keep our family relationships in working order, staying in good contact, relationships at work go better also.*

Even brief contact, when time is limited, can work wonders for functioning. A colleague told of going to a distant city to speak. There was a great deal of apprehension. Before the meeting, he called a cousin who lived in the area. They had a brief conversation. He went on to the meeting without any anxiety, continuing to give his talk with unusual calm. Such is the power of connection with the family system.

3. Manage emotional processes, especially in meetings.

As we've seen, emotional processes in meetings can be managed in two ways, by managing emotional process within self and by structuring meetings so the group members are less emotionally triggering to each other.

If the leader of a meeting is calm, focused and connected, the group will most often follow suit. The leader sets the emotional pace and people generally go along with it. Calm is catching, just as is anxiety.

Secondly, if leaders in meetings "chair" it and ask everyone to speak with them, taking turns, not interrupting and speaking only to the chair, his or her calm and thinking attitude has more of a chance to prevail with each instead of what other, less mature members of the group may be bringing to it. Also, the group can listen and hear each other better when they are observing this interaction. It affords more thought, less emotional reactivity. This structuring may be unnecessary in an exceptionally high level, calm group.

Rev. H did not chair the main governing board of his church. He found that because of the way group emotional process operated there, that he did not have the time he needed as the pastor of the congregation, to keep the board apprised of his thinking and activities. He came up with a creative solution that all agreed was needed and would be useful: "The Pastor's Report." It was given at the beginning of the agenda and discussed before any other business. He used it not only for reporting but for defining his best thinking in a thoughtful way to the group. In this way he had a vehicle to communicate from basic self to the board, a most useful activity for any leader and for any organization fortunate enough to have this kind of leader.

If emotional process of groups in the congregation are seen as a fact of human existence that can be understood, rather than something to be feared or dreaded, its workings can be approached in a thinking way for the better functioning of small working groups as well as for the larger congregation.

4. Don't be afraid to say "No" to the immaturity.

Of course, a certain amount of immature behavior is expected, inevitable and harmless in any group, since no group has one hundred per cent of members at "100" on the scale. But, more and more, in contemporary congregations, the immature members seem to band together, (people at similar levels on the scale attract) go off on tangents and wreak havoc. When this happens, rather than putting immature members in charge of committees and boards, boundaries need to be set and limits defined. How one goes about this is the question.

Pastor C, in the beginning, was courted and made to feel extremely valued and welcomed by a small "in" group of the congregation who socialized frequently together. Within months, however, this positive flipped to negative. The group insisted on doing its own thing—for example, it ran a service in ways that the worship committee and pastor had not approved. Sometimes other members were ridiculed or made fun of in presentations in ways that made clear who they were referring to. Sometimes they planned meetings or put up signs that had not been approved through appropriate channels. If the pastor objected to this behavior, one or more of them would literally scream in her face. After these episodes, Rev. C would become extremely anxious and unable to sleep for several days. Her emotional health began to suffer. She lost concentration and lived in fear of meeting one of the "in" group in the church hallways, which they frequented.

As she started to apply family systems principles to the situations, she realized that *she had the equivalent of emotionally rebellious teenagers on her hands.* Though she liked to be liked, she would have to learn to say "no" and accept that she couldn't please all of the people all of the time. She discussed the situation with the more mature leadership of appropriate committees. They had known for a long time that the whole congregation was suffering by this state of affairs. They were all being held hostage by a small group, and were very tired of the situation.

From that time on, as incidents occurred, Pastor C would take them to the committee leadership involved and together they would approach the offenders, saying "no" in kind but firm ways. They were informed that their behavior was unacceptable and had to stop. This process was repeated whenever necessary, which turned out to be often. At the same time, members of the "in" group were removed, gradually, from leadership positions.

They did not like being said "no" to. They did not like being removed from positions of leadership. When the pastor and other leaders were screamed at they replied calmly, but if it continued, they were asked to continue the conversation at another time. In time the ring leaders left. Without them the "in" group was much less intense. There were fewer incidents. The church functioned much better over all. Pastor C experienced being more of a self in all her relationships. She became recognized as someone who knew how to handle "difficult" congregations.

In an anxious society, there are more anxious people. They are adopting postures of rebelliousness, stirring conflict, distance, and all the other relationship patterns. As Extraordinary Leaders relate out of theoretical guidelines, they find they have direction. The congregational leaders are also there to assist.

5. Choose your emotional tone.

The ability to choose one's own emotional state, not allowing it to be determined by that of other people, is part of being a high level leader. Most of us will have to work hard at that one since emotional states in general are quite infectious. But it is the mark of a high level of differentiation.

Whenever Rev. D became aware of critical, rumor-mongering, agitated members, he had a wonderful way of handling these situations. He did not crouch into a corner and pout. He approached the person, asking him to come see him. When he came in, as he described it, he simply listened calmly, with interest. He said, "I don't explain, justify or defend, I just listen. And when the anxiety has run down, I make no promises, I sincerely thank the person for coming in to talk with me and giving me the benefit of his or her thinking." Usually the rumors and criticism stop. If not, he repeats the process from time to time. In time they learned to come to him in the beginning rather than broadcasting anxiety around the congregation.

This minister was expert at keeping his own emotional state where he wanted it to be, regardless of that of others—a high level leader, to be sure.

6. In a regressive society, you may be different.

In anxious times, when immature behavior is the order of the day and seems to be in control, people act according to ill-thought-through or not-at-all-thought-through guidelines. When they encounter a leader with well thought-through principles who behaves according to them, there will be a clash. Most leaders today are ill-equipped to take a stand. Or the stands they do take are based on emotion or relationships rather than guiding principles.

So clergy today, like school principles who again are finding dress codes necessary, may find they often don't agree with prevalent behavior and mores. It is inevitable, logically, that high level leaders in times of societal regression will have to define themselves. They may not fit the mold if they're working on building more basic self. But they know where they stand. They are not at the mercy of shifting fads and unfounded ideas.

7. Be a relationship master.

Bowen theory, with its clear guidelines for relationships goes further to assist leaders than any other way of thinking of which this author is aware.

As they are practiced, equality, openness and separateness become more a way of life, needing to be worked at less. The relationship functioning that these guiding principles establish, mean that most of the leadership snafus we hear about frequently simply don't come about. Most leadership difficulties come about as a result of the way the leader interacts with others.

If he or she is thinking and relating openly in the system, defining self from basic principles will naturally happen from time to time. Sometimes these "step-ups" will be applauded. Sometimes brickbats will fly.[1] The Extraordinary Leader knows that either an over-positive or an over-negative reaction is a potential togetherness trap. If one stays on course though, guided

---

[1] Bowen used to refer to brickbats this way: "I guess when the brickbats stop flying, I'll know I'm done."

by principle and defining self to the group when appropriate, it is a pleasure to see how the group will, over time, come up to meet one in functioning.

Thinking It Over

Keeping the focus on self management, Extraordinary Leaders make time for the staff and volunteer leadership of the organization, one-on-one and regularly. They tend their family relationships. They know how to manage emotional process in meetings. They can say "no" when necessary and they can ask for help. Addressing people and issues from basic self, they expect not always to be liked. They can keep their own emotional state separate from others.

Real Life Research

1. What are some common traps Extraordinary Leaders can fall into?

2. What are some that are laid for them?

3. Why are one's own family relationships important?

4. Why isn't the Extraordinary Leader always liked?

5. What are some possible ways to manage not being liked?

6. Who would you ask for help in an intense take-over situation?

7. Who would you try to keep out of leadership positions in a congregation?

8. What would you look for in suggesting people for leadership positions?

9. In what areas do you need to define self in your systems?

10. What are some leadership pitfalls that family systems principles could have helped you out of?

Epilogue—And Some Surprises

Last summer, I was invited to be a part of the annual Lake Junaluska leadership training session for new leadership in a large denomination. It was almost exactly thirty years after Dr. Karl Menninger had been there. He had reported in his book, *Whatever Became of Sin?*, that he went to Lake Junaluska to learn what he could from clergy trainers about the problems being encountered. He learned that clergy people were disenfranchised, confused, lacking direction, and exhausted.

During various breaks, I took the opportunity to speak with bishops and others in high positions in the denomination, asking them the same question Dr. Menninger had asked 30 years earlier: "What did they see as major problems of the clergy?" I received very similar answers. One bishop was particularly articulate: "They come out of seminary excited, enthusiastic, well equipped and ready to fulfill their call. They can't wait. And they do pretty well for awhile. But sometime during their years in ministry, they hit a wall. They lose their passion. All the steam goes out of them. Many would like to leave at this point but they have a retirement incentive to stay. So they stay, but they're not very effective. I believe the whole church suffers as a result of this phenomenon."

(Some have thought about this and seen, as the answer, to help them out of the ministry, fitting them for another vocation. Perhaps there are some who were ill-fitted for the ministry to begin with.)

Many clergy people have described this "wall" to me also. Sometimes it is defined as a spiritual crisis. When I listen to the details of the stories brought to me, I think it is not so much spiritual, though people often tell of not being able to pray, or being mad at God. *As I hear it, these pastors have been ill prepared for their encounter with the emotional side of the congregation.* Their bishops, presbyters, superintendents, and other officers are similarly ill prepared, so they have no idea about how to coach them through their difficulties.

Theory shows the way out, as we have seen. Once they have a way of managing themselves through the intensities, their enthusiasm and energy return. They know what to do, how to think. Their spiritual crisis is often over as well. They step up to a higher level of functioning.

Surprises

Some of the surprise lessons the clergy taught me, which caught me unaware, follow:

- Clergy learn to think systems and apply the ideas faster than any group I have taught.

- Clergy counseling is important and can accomplish much more than I ever thought.

- Large systems are also emotional systems after all.

- The clergy are not alone in dealing with the immaturity of the group.

- The officials are lost and need a compass, too.

1. Clergy learn to think systems fast.

Of all the categories of people I have interacted within thinking systems—parents, educators, therapists, business people—clergy are by far the most apt in learning the family systems theory ideas and applying them. Many people have offered suggestions as to why this is the case—possibly they see the need because they work daily in emotional systems and have come up against them, maybe they are smarter, or perhaps it is that they work with families all the time. I am sure all these factors may be playing a part, but the phenomenon is still a bit of a mystery to me.

A clergy person, in only the second coaching session, returned to tell of how he had learned about his overfunctioning posture to his wife in the first session. He did things differently with her beginning the next day. He returned, full of enthusiasm, describing how much better the relationship already was functioning.

A number of others, whose wives had become so depressed they could not function, found, after they stopped having the answers for their spouses, defined self and took more of an equal posture, that their wives' depressions disappeared.

These are the kind of results therapists dream of, but rarely see.

Of course, if people are doing better at home, it is easier to do well at work. And,

If you know theory, you can use it. If you don't, you can't.

2. Clergy counseling is important.

One clergy person surprised me with a paper that described her counseling with one family on the brink of divorce. She had, by bringing her knowledge of family systems theory to bear with this couple, literally saved the marriage. And this happened in only six sessions with the family

Others, caring too much about certain members or leadership roles in their congregations, found that when they took a less overfunctioning posture, showing more confidence, a more relaxed, equal posture, the members did better in their leadership roles or simply as members, needing less clergy time.

3. Large systems are emotional systems too.

I used to say that small congregations are emotional units but I wasn't sure about large ones. After all, many of the people in large groups don't even know one another.

But a clergy person in the seminar offered: "I think large systems are emotional systems. My evidence is that since I have begun to work on myself, my whole congregation is much calmer, there are less problems to deal with and the congregation is cooperatively working together much better. So, if a group stepping up in functioning is evidence that they are an emotional system, I think that large groups are emotional systems too." His congregation was over 600 strong.

4. Clergy are not alone in dealing with the immaturity.

The clergy taught me that, when needed, there is other leadership in the congregation, ready and willing to assist when the immaturity has to be addressed. Just as it takes two parents, optimally, to rear children, there are others in the congregation—the maturity and strength of the congregation—who can be counted on to join hands with the clergy in setting limits and defining boundaries. They can be the "other parent" for the clergy person. Usually they only have to be asked. They are tired of certain negative situations too, and are only too willing to take part in addressing them. If they are called on, the church works better—the clergy person encourages the cooperation that a congregation needs in order to be effective, as people step up to bat, taking more responsible stances. But the clergy leader has to take the initial "I" position.

Clergy, while they do need to be as clear-thinking as possible, and able to take a stand when necessary, don't have to take all the responsibility for how the group functions. They have partners within the system that are ready to help, when asked, in addressing the immaturity.

5. Officials are lost, needing a compass, too.

From what the clergy are telling me, I can see that their supervisors and superior officers in their organizations rarely have a clue as to how to advise them or coach them when in difficult, emotionally-based situations. If I ask them, in tough situations, what their next-in-command thought, they often reply, "Oh, I wouldn't want to go to him or her. I have tried that and got only a very busy, rushed response that wasn't very useful." They seem to be too busy to listen at all most of the time."

Though there are a few officers of the church and synagogue who are gifted in knowing how to coach clergy persons when they are stuck with relationship and emotional systems problems, they are few and far between. For the most part, it seems to me that "being too busy" for certain critical situations or people, is a cover for not knowing any directions for handling oneself in a system when anxiety rises.

Bishops, (or their equivalents in different denominations) whose major role, I thought, was "pastor of the pastor," function as such in only a proportion of instances that I hear about. What is usual, when a disgruntled parishioner calls the bishop to complain, is that the bishop sides with the immaturity and takes sides against the clergy person. Officers, it seems, often have no way of thinking about emotional neutrality in situations like this. They have no way of knowing how to coach the ministers. For example, they rarely refer the persons back to the clergy person, or refuse to discuss the minister when he or she is not present. They, like other officers of church and synagogue, have no guidebook and compass to direct them through intense systems. Usually their own anxiety, lack of knowledge about systems and crowded schedule combine to mean that a great number of situations are mishandled. Then too, they sometimes act as bureaucrats, seeing emotional systems symptoms as of low priority and importance.

If they did know better how to coach clergy when appropriate about the emotional side of a congregation, they would save the church a great deal of trouble and often, expense. Some officers of denominations are beginning to present themselves for didactic learning and for coaching.[1] So perhaps there may be hope for the future.

---

[1] In this, a great boost has been given by the Rev. Dr. Gwen Purushotham in the Office of the General Board of Higher Education and Ministry of the National Conference of the United Methodist Church, who has helped to make attendance at the Extraordinary Leadership Seminar possible for District Superintendents.

Further Guidelines

People get extremely excited about learning to think systems and after awhile often make the mistake of thinking that they know it, now, and don't need further contact with the ideas, at one extreme, or that they are an authority, at the other.

Some write, teach and publish too soon. Perhaps we all do. I wish people could dampen their enthusiasm for this most useful way of thinking long enough to get a good solid understanding under their belt *before* they start to publish and teach. Many teachers, trainees, and coaches are teaching Bowen theory, having received all their education from books, even though there are wonderful centers in their areas where they could obtain didactic and coaching experiences. It is unfortunate to see people reaching only a small portion of what they are capable. I also see much erosion of theory happening in this way. A little learning can be dangerous.

Learning to think systems is not just a case of "getting the idea," going to the meetings now and then, or taking a seminar or two. It is a continuing process and a lot of work on self in one's systems. As far as I can tell, those of us who are serious about thinking systems, need to stay in touch with others thinking systems, attend meetings, listen to case studies, the rest of our lives. I do. I meet with colleagues on a regular basis in order to keep my head thinking systems and out of "cause and effect" thinking, blame, and individual thinking. *All of us revert to these modes unless there is special effort to prevent ourselves from turning back to more automatic ways of thinking.* I see people coming in and out of the seminar and other training programs I am connected with, making what seems to be a serious effort, but not continuing to stay connected with the ideas. I believe they will lose their ability to think systems if they don't find a way to continue to think with others who are advanced in them. For this reason, there are advanced seminars and conferences where people can continue to think systems.

The Big Surprise

The biggest surprise of all, as I look back on it, is my "going into" this teaching/coaching ministry at all! Had the Methodist Virginia Conference Leadership Development Institute[2] not seen a vision for a program, approached me more than once, and supported it in every way possible,[3] this rich experience would not have taken place. But the invitation was providential. Life can sometimes be planned and planned for, but there are always some total surprises for all of us. I never dreamed I would be ministering to ministers. But doing so has been and continues to be the most exciting, interesting and gratifying imaginable mission to which to devote my life energy.

In case the point has not yet been made in these pages, I want to echo and emphasize what Dr. Menninger, many years ago seemed to be emphasizing in his writing:[4] *The clergy are society's most important profession.* They are much more important than they realize. When and as they begin to

---

[2] The office was led, at that time, by Rev.Lucy Marsden Hottle, who originally had the vision for the program, inspiring me to plan and develop it.

[3] The Virginia Methodist Conference has, from the beginning, with Lucy Marsden Hottle's initial idea and tireless encouragement, supported the program with generous grants for tuition. She and her husband actually transport clergy people to and from the airport when needed. Others have seen the value of the seminar and done much to advance its growth: Rev. Beth Downs in the Office of Ministerial Services of the Board of Ordained Ministry of the Virginia Conference of the United Methodist Church, has continued to actively support the program in many ways. The Rev. Dr. Gwen Purushotham of the General Board of Higher Education and Ministry at the Virginia Conference's national level, has made the program available to District Superintendents of the Methodist Church. Rev. Tom Hay, Executive Presbyter in the Shenandoah Valley Presbytery, devoted many hours to planning for the Shenandoah Valley Seminar and, then, in interesting Presbyterian clergy in attending. Rev. Carl Dickerson and Rev. Jerry Foust have each initiated new seminars in two different areas. Rev. Carl Dickerson interested the United Methodist denomination at the national level in the program.

[4] See Menninger, *op cit.*

understand that fact, they have the possibility now, as they have through history, of significantly impacting society for the better.

I am most blessed and privileged to be able to assist them as they perform their vital missions.

Acknowledgements

Thank You To . . .

Dr. Murray Bowen, to whom so many are indebted for seeing "the family as an emotional unit," as well as the myriad of other concepts and ideas that flowed out of that, for mentoring me and all of my coaches and teachers.

Mrs. Leroy Bowen and Dr. Joanne Bowen who have supported me, read manuscripts and encouraged me in my work over the years.

Dr. Michael Kerr and the faculty of the Bowen Center for the Study of the Family, my colleagues, who continue to teach Bowen theory, each in his or her own special way. Each brings a world of different thinking and experience to the ideas that always shows their rich application to all of life and never fails to inform and give new light.

Rev. Lucy Marsden Hottle, Dean of the Leadership Development Institute of the Virginia Annual Conference of the United Methodist Church originally saw the need and had the idea for Extraordinary Leadership Seminar, promoted it by setting up promotional meetings, guiding it through the many committees needed, finding money for clergy scholarships, guiding people to the seminar and for her continued interest in it.

All the clergy participants in the seminar, who have learned complex ideas with great rapidity, and have taught as much as they have learned.

Rev. Beth Downs, Director of Ministerial Services of the Board of Ordained Ministry, of the Virginia Conference of the United Methodist Church, who has supported the seminar in every way possible.

Rev. Carl Dickerson, who originally invited the seminar to Pensacola, FL, where it had a warm, wonderful home until the hurricanes made it move. He also interested the national office of his denomination in the seminars.

The Rev. Dr. Gwen Purushotham, who has enthusiastically promoted the seminar at the national level of the United Methodist Church, making it possible for district superintendents to attend the program.

Rev. Jerry Foust who saw the need for a new seminar in the Shenandoah Valley and worked hard to interest other leaders, making it happen.

Rev. Tom Hay, Executive Presbyter of the Shenandoah Valley, who responded to Rev. Foust's request, working along with him and other clergy in the area to create the Shenandoah Seminar.

Kathleen Cotter Cauley, whose eyes sparkled with enthusiasm when she heard of the seminar. She has not missed one since that day, and has contributed as a dedicated faculty member, from her rich knowledge and experience, taking more responsibility for the success of the seminar as time goes by.

Rev. Kenton Derstine, the newest faculty member, whose excitement about the seminar led him to find its third section's home in the Eastern Mennonite Seminary, and for promoting and producing his thoughtful lectures and coaching based on his long term knowledge of and experience with Bowen theory.

Dr. Joseph Douglass, whose outstanding editing, writing and publishing ability, took the manuscript and made it into a usable book. His gentle spirit in the midst of computer-triggered tantrums found a way out of many an emotional thicket. And, he cooks. How blessed can a person be?

Appendix I

Glossary Of Terms Used In Bowen Family Systems Theory

Anxiety Usually defined as "the response of the organism to real or imagined threat." Clinical experience at different levels of differentiation of self suggests that anxiety is so continuously present in life, so much a fact of the individual's and family's patterns as to be stimulated in other ways as well. Anxiety can simply be "caught" from others even though there is no threat or imagined threat situation.

Another definition may therefore be proposed: *heightened reactivity.* Anxiety may be a reaction to stressors from outside the family system or the person or it may be generated from inside the system or from within the person. It may be chronic—passed along in a family system for years or even generations. It may be acute—relatively short-term. The effects of anxiety in a system are multiple: generally an increase of togetherness is evidenced by more triangling and other relationship postures. Physical, mental, emotional or social symptoms of any intensity can occur at any level of differentiation, given enough anxiety. Anxiety is manifest in quantitative changes in the body that include cells, organs and organ systems, as well as thought and behavioral expressions and patterns.

Basic Self The differentiated or emotionally mature part of the self. It is guided by carefully thought-out principles that form an inner guidance system. Basic self is non-negotiable. That is, it is not given up to other selves in relationships nor is it added to by other selves in a relationship. Therefore, its boundaries are "impermeable". It is distinguished from the pseudo, or functional self, which has more permeable boundaries, and can be added to or given up in relationships with the pseudoselves of others. The functional self functions better in favorable circumstances and relationships and less well in adverse conditions. Basic self, because of its inner guidance system and less permeable boundaries, is always more reliable for best thinking, decision making and directing behavior. People higher on the scale of differentiation have more basic self, whereas people lower on the scale have less basic self.

Differentiation of Self. As a noun, a way of thinking about the variation in functioning of humans and higher mammals. People all have differing abilities to adapt—that is, to deal with the exigencies of life, live a goal directed life of achievement. The word "differentiation" derives from the science of embryology. In the developing fetus groups of cells that are identical in the beginning, "differentiate" from each other in order to form the different organs of the body. People fall along a theoretical spectrum of differentiation—"the scale of differentiation of self"—according to their unresolved emotional attachments to their parents (and to some degree, their siblings). Indices of differentiation include physical health and abilities, relationship success, intelligence, vocational success, social skills and emotional maturity. People range from very high levels of differentiation (theoretical "100" on the scale) of self to very low levels, (theoretical "0" on the scale) depending on how much basic self is present. People at higher levels, those with more basic self, tend toward more overall success in life, both vocationally and in their relationships. They also tend towards less physical, mental/emotional and social symptoms. The more basic self a person attains, the more inner direction he or she has and the more choice at any given time regarding whether to operate out of emotions or intellect. People at higher levels function more often out of their principles (these are well thought-out) than do people at lower levels.

People at lower levels have less choice between thinking and emotions: their behavior patterns are more emotion-based and automatic. Emotion-based patterns include compliance, rebelliousness and fear of rejection. Lower level individuals also have more attachment needs than do those at higher levels. Differentiation of self has a rough equivalence with emotional maturity, though it has nothing to do with chronological age. It is a broader concept, taking in all the areas of functioning of an individual, including the physical health.

The concept contains a set of rather detailed principles which, when implemented, lead not only to improved emotional and relationship functioning, but also in all other spheres. There is a direct correlation between level of differentiation and amount of basic self. At higher levels of differentiation, a greater amount of basic self exists and at lower levels, a smaller amount.

As an action word, a verb, differentiation of self is the continued project of people who work with family systems theory. [18]

Emotional maturity The ability of the individual to manage the emotional part of the self in an adaptive way. In a more mature person, long term goals and benefits will be given priority over short term ones when they conflict. A similar concept to differentiation of self, it is not as inclusive. (See also differentiation of self.)

Emotional System The emotional unit, a group of individuals who, by virtue of time spent together are involved in meaningful relationships. This might include groupings of other species, the human family (nuclear or extended) or a workplace system. Emotions circulate from individual to individual by means of

---

[18] The useful distinction between differentiation as noun and as verb was first made by Kathleen Kerr, in lectures and comments over the years, at the Bowen Center.

patterned emotional reactions—distance, conflict, over- and underfunctioning, and triangling.

This term may also refer to the emotional system within an individual; that is, the part of the nervous system and organs involved in emotional responses. For instance, a perception of danger may involve sense organs, such eyes and ears, reptilian or limbic brain centers, the hypothalamus alerting the adrenals, the adrenal glands secreting adrenalin, raising blood pressure and increasing cardiac output, as well as many other physiologic responses that make a fight or flight response possible.

Emotions The instinctual, automatic forces that operate in animals and thus, in human beings. Examples of these forces are territoriality and procreation, found in reptiles as well as more complex species, or nurturance of the young and play, found only in higher mammals. These reactions have an insistent quality. They originate in the various parts of the midbrain associated with these functions and are carried out by the individual's "emotional system," the brain-nervous system-end organs complex involved in the emotion. Emotions also include fight-or-flight reactions and patterned reactions, which get set in the developing organism with repetition.

Feelings Emotions, or automatic responses that are in awareness.

Fusion Emotional attachment of two or more selves for which the mother/child symbiosis is a paradigm. It can be seen in any intense important relationship, however. Both selves in a fusion are intensely emotionally reactive to each other and experience a loss or gain of self in the relationship.

Inner Guidance System See Basic Self.

Nuclear Family Emotional System See Emotional System.

Pseudo self The part of self that is negotiated in a relationship. It is more reactive, less prone to think before acting and less guided by principle. It is also determined more by the environment, especially relationships, than by the self.

Reactivity The tendency of the organism to respond to perceived threat or the anxiety of others. It is more pronounced at lower levels of differentiation.

Scale of Differentiation of Self An imaginary continuum (from theoretical "0" to theoretical "100") upon which all human beings fall, from the most differentiated to the least. A person may appear to function at a high level but if those in his or her emotional unit are not, he or she is probably gaining pseudoself from them, (gaining self at the expense of the functioning of others in the system) and so cannot be considered to actually possess the high level that is apparent.

Level of differentiation can be properly assessed only by of observation of an entire lifetime and by taking into consideration the levels of important others. The effect of circumstances shows itself on the pseudoself, not the basic self. (See also Differentiation)

Self See Basic Self.

Symbiosis A mutually dependent emotional attachment between two people. The concept comes from biology where two organisms are dependent upon each other for survival. (The human, for example, lives in symbiosis with certain bacteria present in the gastrointestinal tract. The bacteria, being fed by the human's food, produce vitamin K, essential for the clotting of blood.) In the family, individuals who fuse selves into relationships emotionally can be thought of as being in an emotional symbiosis. To the degree that the symbiosis is resolved, or grown away from, during maturation, the individual is said to have differentiated a self. To the degree that the original tendency toward symbiosis remains, differentiation of self is incomplete and the self is vulnerable to forming other emotionally dependent relationships.

System The emotional relationships between or among individual human beings or individuals of other species. Usually all that is needed for individuals to become emotionally significant, or important to each other is for them to spend a significant amount of time with one another. When individuals spend a significant amount of time together, they will begin, sooner or later, to trigger each other emotionally and the phenomenon of "passing" anxiety from one to another, in patterns, can be observed. These phenomena are more pronounced, the lower on the scale of differentiation the group and less so, the higher on the scale.

Triangle Three individuals emotionally related to each other start to pass their anxiety to each other, or "triangle." Triangles are the building blocks of emotional systems. Emotional intensity takes place alternately among the different pairs forming the triangle; anxiety travels around it. In each family system there are many triangles, some of which reach out to society at large by way of friendship systems or agencies of society. In this way, society itself is built of interlocking triangles.

Words Outlawed in Extraordinary Leadership Seminars:

> Bowenian
> Genogram
> Healthy
> Self-differentiation
> Sick
> Systemic
> Triangulate or Triangulation

Appendix II

Bibliography of Recommended Readings in Bowen Theory

Bowen, Murray: *Family Therapy in Clinical Practice,* Jason and Aronson, New York, 1978. A collection of Bowen's papers. Now published by Rowman and Littlefield.

Family Systems, a Journal of Psychiatry and the Natural Sciences, Order from Bowen Center for the Study of the Family, 4400 MacArthur Blvd., Washington, D.C. 202-965-4400.

Gilbert, Roberta *Extraordinary Relationships, A New Way of Thinking About Human Interactions.* John Wiley and Sons, New York, 1992. An entry level guide to the use of Bowen family systems theory to improve relationships.

Gilbert, Roberta *Connecting With Our Children: Principles for Parents in a Troubled World* John Wiley and Sons, New York, 1999 An Introduction to Bowen theory for parents.

Gilbert, Roberta *The Eight Concepts of Bowen Theory*, Leading Systems Press, Basye and Falls Church, VA, 2004

Hall, Margaret *Bowen Family Systems Theory and its Uses* Jason and Aronson, New York. A sociologist's perspective.

Kerr, Michael and Bowen, Murray *Family Evaluation* W. W. Norton and Co., New York, 1988 Written for therapists but read by and useful to everyone.

Papero, Daniel *Bowen Family Systems Theory,* Allyn and Bacon, Needham Heights, Mass, 1990, A primer of Bowen family systems Theory

Rosenbaum, Lillian, *Biofeedback Frontiers,* AMS Press New York, 1989

Titleman, Peter, ed. *Clinical Applications of Bowen Family Systems Theory,* Haworth Press, New York, 1998 An edited book by many experienced contributors.

Titelman, Peter, ed. *Emotional Cutoff,* Haworth Press, New York, 2003 Many contributions from experienced systems thinkers.

Toman, Walter *Family Constellation, Its Effects of Personality and Social Behavior* Springer Publishing Co. New York 1961 Toman's account of his seminal work on sibling position.

Sagar, R ed. *Understanding Organizations,* The Bowen Center 4400 MacArthur Blvd, Washington D.C. 20007, 202-965-4400 www.thebowencenter.org

Appendix III

Teaching and Training Centers in Bowen Theory

California

Programs in Bowen Theory
Contact: Laura Havstad
120 Pleasant Hill Ave. No #370
Sebastapol, CA 95472
Phone/fax: 707-823-1848
Website: www.programsinbowentheory.org
Email: info@programsinbowentheory.org

Southern California Training in Bowen Theory and Psychotherapy
Contact: Carolyn Jacobs, Psy.D.
625 Third Avenue
Chula Vista, CA 91910
Phone: 619-525-7747
Fax: 619-476- 7566
Website: www.sctbt.homestead.com
Email: sctbt@cox.net

Canada

Living Systems
Contact: Randall Frost, Director of Training and Research
1500 Marine Drive
North Vancouver, British Columbia
Canada V7P1T7
Phone: 604-926-5496
Fax: 604-904-5141
Website:www.livingsystems.ca
Email: livingsystems@telus.net

Florida

Florida Family Research Network
Contact: Eileen Gottlieb, M.Ed., LMFT
    Shelly Fine, MA, LMHC
    Constance Fitzgerald, M.D.
    Jeff Miller, LCSW
    Vicky Topcik, M.Ed., LMHC
    Kathleen Keating Yanks RN, MS, CS-P
232 SW 28th Avenue
DelRay FL 33445
Phone: 561-279-0861
Fax: 561-243-6838
Email: ebgfamilycenter@adelphia.net

Illinois

Center for Family Consultation
Contact: Robert Noone, PhD
    Sydney Reed MSW
    Carol Moran MSW
    Stephanie Ferrera MSW
820 Davis St. Suite 218
Evanston IL 60201
Phone: 847-475-1221
bnoone@ren.com

Iowa

Des Moines Bowen Family Systems Theory Study Group
Contact: David Drake D.O.
1221 Center Street Ste 3
Des Moines IO 50309-1014
515-288-8000

Kansas

Bowen Family Systems Clinical Seminars
Contact: Peg Donley, MSW
    Carroll Hoskins, MSW
7301 Mission Road, Suite 310
Prairie Village, KS 66208

Phone: 913-722-1010

Prairie Center for Family Therapy
Contact: Tamara Hawk LSCSW
210 Southwind Place #1B
Manhattan, KS 66503
Phone/Fax: 785-539-7789
Website: www.theprairiecenter.com
Email: tjhawk@cox.net

Massachusetts

New England Seminar on Bowen Theory
Contact: Ann V. Nicholson, RNCS,
    Peter Titelman, Ph. D.
Worcester Mass
Phone: 617-296-4614
Email: ann.nicholson@verizon.net

Missouri

KC Center for Family and Organizational Systems
Contact: Margaret Otto, MSW
        Kathy Riordan, MSW
3100 NE 83rd St. Suite 2350
Kansas City MO 64119
Phone: 816-436-1180
       816-436-1721
Website: www.kcfamilysystems.com

New Jersey

Princeton Family Center
Contact: Selden Dunbar Illick LCSW
    Candace Jones LCSW
    Joan McElroy LCSW
Box 573
4422 Main Street
Kingston NJ 08528
Phone: 609-924-0514
www.princetonfamilycenter.org

Pennsylvania

Western Pennsylvania Family Center
733 North Highland Avenue
Pittsburgh, PA 15206
Phone: 412-362-2295
Fax: 412-363-2489
www.wpfc.net

Texas

Center for the Study of Natural Systems and the Family
Contact: Victoria Harrison, MA (Houston)
      Michael Quinn, 512--482-1998(Austin)
      Louise Rauseo, 443-623-4012 (El Paso)
PO Box 701187
Houston, Texas 77027-1187
Phone: 713-790-0226
Website: www.csnsf.org
Email: vaharrison@sbcglobal.net

Family Health Services
Contact: Victoria Harrison, MA
729 Rutland St.
Houston, TX 77007
Phone: 713-790-0226
Email: vaharrison@sbcglobal.net

Vermont

Workplace Solutions
Contact: Gordon Petersen, MSW, LICSW, CEAP
  66 Battery St.
  Burlington, VT 05401
  Phone: 802-862-3373
  e-mail: Workplaz@together.net

The Vermont Center for Family Studies
Contact: Anne Bunting PhD
    Phone: 802-863-5536
    e-mail: anndb@gmavt.net
    Monica Baege, EdD, LCMHC
    Phone: 802-872-1818

e-mail: monika.baege@uvm.edu
Mercy Russell Hyde, MSW
Phone: 802-233-1142
e-mail: mercy@russellhyde.net
Gordon Petersen, MSW, LICSW, CEAP
Phone: 802-862-3373
Erik Thompson MA
Phone:802-658-4800
e-mail: erikt@wcmhs.org
Burlington, VT

Virginia

Center for the Study of Human Systems
Contact: Roberta Gilbert M.D.
     Kathleen Cotter Cauley LMFT
     Kenton Derstine M.Div
Falls Church, VA 22046
Phone: 703-532-3823
Website: www.hsystems.org
Email: rgoffice313@verizon.com

Shenandoah Valley Family Systems Network
Contact: Janis Norton, LCSW
     Elaine Dunaway, LCSW
     Donna Van Horn, LCSW
     Kenton Derstine, M Div
     Roberta Gilbert, MD
Email: janisnorton@verizon.net
Website: www.shenfamilysystemsnetwork.org

Washington, D.C.

Bowen Center for the Study of the Family
Contact: Marjorie Hottel
4400 MacAurthur Blvd. NW
Washington D.C.
Phone: 202-965-4400
Website: www.thebowencenter.org
Email information for individuals on website

Leaders for Tomorrow, Inc.
Contact: Andrea Maloney Schara
4545 42nd St. NW Suite 201
Washington D.C. 20016
Phone: 202-966-1145, 703-598-5953
E-mail: arms711@aol.com

The Learning Space
Contact: Priscilla J. Friesen, LICSW
    Regina P. Carrick, LPC
    Glennon T. Gordon, LICSW
4545 42nd St. NW #201
Washington, D.C. 20016
Phone: 202-966-1145
Fax: 202-966-2265

Working Systems
Contact: Kathy Wiseman
4545 42nd St. NW Suite 201
Washington DC 20016
Phone 202 244 6481
       202 812 1449 cell
       202 966 2265 fax
www.AWorkingSystem.com

INDEX

Dr. Roberta Gilbert

is a psychiatrist in Falls Church, Virginia. She divides her time between teaching and directing at the Center for the Study of Human Systems, private practice in Falls Church, Virginia, and faculty responsibilities and teaching at the Bowen Center for the Study of the Family at Georgetown in Washington, D.C. She is one of the leaders in Bowen family systems theory and developer of Extraordinary Leadership Seminars.

The Center for the Study of Human Systems
313 Park Avenue, Suite 308, Falls Church, VA, 22046
www.hsystems.org   Phone 703-532-3823

The Center's mission is to make the knowledge and benefits of Bowen family systems theory as widely available as possible. It disseminates information and organizes seminars and leadership training programs for parents, clergy, and organizational leaders.

The Center began in 1998 when Dr. Gilbert was asked by a major denomination to develop a leadership program for clergy based on Bowen family system theory. *Extraordinary Leadership Seminars* has been growing since then. It focuses on improved individual functioning and leadership effectiveness. Seminars take place one full day a month or for three days three times a year for those from afar, October through June over a three-year cycle. They are led by Dr. Gilbert and other experienced faculty members. For more information, visit the web site www.hsystems.org or contact the Center at 703-532-3823.